100 YEARS
OF AMERICAN CARS

Publications International, Ltd.

Special thanks to the following manufacturers who supplied imagery.

Fisker, Inc.; Ford Motor Company; General Motors Company; Lucid Motors; Nu Ride Inc.; Rivian Automotive, Inc.; Shelby American; Stellantis; Tesla, Inc.

Additional images from Auburn Cord Duesenberg Automobile Museum; Scott Baxter; Ken Beebe; Les Bidrawn; Joe Bohovic; Terry Boyce; Scott Brant; Michael Brown; Chan Bush; Thomas Cannell; Joseph Caro; Jeff Cohn; Deer Park Winery & Auto Museum; Jim Frenak; Diane Garnett; Bob Garris; Gene's Studio; Gilmore Car Museum; Tom Glatch; GM Heritage Archive; Ed Goldberger; David Gooley; Sam Griffith; Mike Hastie; Bob Havorka; Jerry Heasley; Alan Hewko; Bill Hill; Scott Hutchinson; Bert Johnson; Bud Juneau; Bill Kanz; Harry Kapsalis; Laurel H. Kenney; Milton Kieft; Kugler Studio; Randy Lorentzen; Dan Lyons; Vince Manocchi; Bill McCall; Tom McGann; Mark McMahon; Doug Mitchel; Mike Mueller; National Automobile Museum; Jerry Naunheim; Bob Nicholson; Morton Oppenheimer; David Patryas; John Peets; Jay Peck; William Schintz; Shutterstock.com; Gary Smith; Robert Sorgatz; Richard Spiegelman; Dan Stockum; Studebaker National Museum; Gerald Sutphin; Rich Szczepanski; Tom Storm; David Talbot; David Temple; Bob Tenney; Marvin Terrell; Thomas Photo; Jim Thompson; Kris Trexler; Rob Van Schaik; Volo Auto Museum; W. C. Waymack; Joseph Wherry; Wieck Media Services; Willoughby Photographic; Hub Wilson; Nicky Wright; Vince Wright; Zoom Photographic

Louis Weber, CEO
Publications International, Ltd.
5250 Old Orchard Road, Suite 500
Skokie, IL 60077

ISBN: 978-1-63938-961-2

Manufactured in China.

8 7 6 5 4 3 2 1

CONTENTS

INTRODUCTION

A RIDE THROUGH HISTORY

For more than a century, the automobile has been at the heart of American culture. From the first mass-produced cars rolling off assembly lines to the powerful muscle cars of the '60s, the gas crises of the '70s, and today's shift toward electrification, each decade has presented unique challenges, innovations, and machines.

100 Years of American Cars takes you on a journey through the evolution of American cars from 1925 to 2025. Each year highlights the best and brightest, while showcasing everything from luxury cruisers and economy compacts to record-breaking performance cars and innovative electric vehicles. Whether you're a longtime enthusiast or simply curious about the cars that shaped America's roads, **100 Years of American Cars** offers a look into the cars that defined their eras.

1925

Ford was still dominating the industry with the Model T, but competitors were catching up. This year saw the rise of more affordable closed-body cars, shifting the market away from open touring models.

New "enclosed" touring cars, with a permanent top and sliding side windows, joined the 1925 Buick line. This $1475 Master Six was one of 160,411 Buicks built for the year.

▲ Angular styling didn't diminish the appeal of the Nash Special Six, which replaced the make's four-cylinder line. This Model 133 two-door sedan, with its 207-cid engine, cost $1225.

▼ Even though the '25 Ford Fordor sold for $660—about twice the price of a touring car—81,050 were sold.

◀ In 1925, the $735 Chevrolet closed coach, with wooden wheels and balloon tires, was a popular family car.

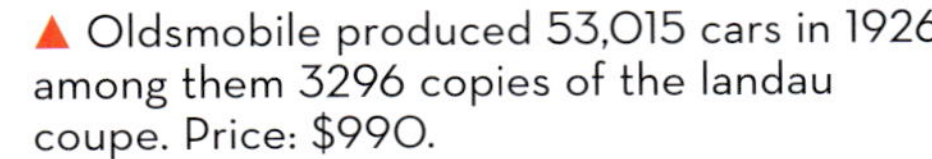

▲ Oldsmobile produced 53,015 cars in 1926, among them 3296 copies of the landau coupe. Price: $990.

◀ The top-selling '27 Chevrolet was the $695 coach: 239,566 units. Closed cars were still growing in popularity.

▶ Two new Hupmobiles arrived in '26: A-1 Six on a 114-inch wheelbase and E-2 Eight on a 125-inch chassis.

▲ In addition to the cars issued under its own name, Nash offered the lower-priced Ajax (*right*) for one year only. It was replaced by the Nash Light Six by 1927, with the same 40-bhp, 170-cid L-head engine. "True" Nashes used overhead-valve sixes.

1926

1926 saw American automakers refining their designs and expanding production. Advancements in engineering and styling set the stage for the rapidly evolving automotive landscape of the late 1920s.

The last of an era: the '27 Ford Model T. More than 15 million had been built. The Model A was next.

1927

Ford finally retired the Model T after 15 million units, shutting down production for months to retool for the all-new Model A. Chevrolet capitalized on the downtime, gaining ground in the sales race.

The five-millionth Chevrolet was a coach—Chevy's top '28 seller by far.

Legendary stylist Harley Earl earned credit for the new 1927 LaSalle, which had a 75-bhp, 303-cid L-head V-8. GM slotted it between Buick and Cadillac.

▲ Prince William of Sweden (*at wheel*) visited the Nash plant in Kenosha, Wisconsin, in 1927. Scandinavian workers presented him with this newly available Nash Ambassador Six (Model 267) four-door Brougham sedan.

▼ A notable feature of the $1635 '27 Velie 60 Royal Sedan was its front door, slanted to match the windshield. Built in Illinois, Velie lasted for two decades: 1909–29.

▼ New Lovejoy hydraulic shock absorbers and a double-drop frame altered the ride and stance of this $1765 Buick Country Club coupe.

▲ Maurice Lichtenstein of Chicago won this Essex Speedabout in a "College Humor" art contest.

▼ For 1927, Oldsmobile bored its little six to 185 cubic inches, upping output to 47 bhp. Deluxe equipment for this $975 30-E roadster included front/rear bumpers; 2342 were sold.

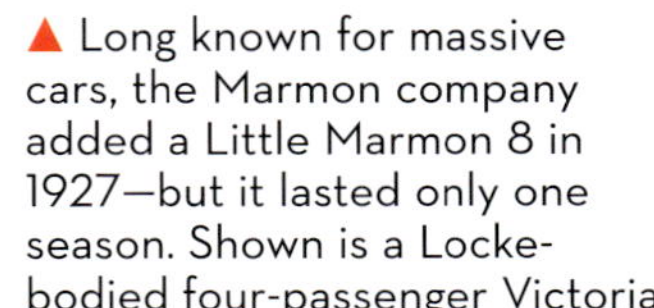

At $1765, buyers couldn't resist this '28 Chevrolet Imperial Landau sedan. This was the first Chevy styled by Harley Earl's Art & Colour Section.

▲ Long known for massive cars, the Marmon company added a Little Marmon 8 in 1927—but it lasted only one season. Shown is a Locke-bodied four-passenger Victoria.

► Crossing the continent with minimal fuel was no problem for the little 1927 Willys-built Whippet four. A Whippet six set a 24-hour endurance record at Indianapolis.

▼ European styling touches flavored the extravagant 1928 Stutz "BB" line, including the Versailles and Biarritz models. Copious racing success earned the brand's lighter Blackhawk model the title of "America's fastest production car."

► Chrysler launched a new marque for 1929: DeSoto. This sharp Roadster Espanol sold for $845. DeSoto's first-year output topped 80,000.

▼ Spare tires moved to front fenders during the Twenties, giving this 1928 LaSalle convertible coupe a dashing air. Model-year LaSalle production came to 14,806 units.

Introduced on August 4, 1928, DeSoto offered seven models on a 109.75-inch wheelbase. All models, including this $845 Phaeton, had hydraulic brakes.

1928

Chrysler introduced the DeSoto brand, offering affordable luxury with advanced engineering. The first DeSoto model boasted a straight-six engine and quickly set sales records.

▲ The top-line 1928 Nash, as before, was the Advanced Six, on a 121- or 127-inch chassis with a 70-bhp, 279-cid six. This $1775 rumble-seat coupe sports paint-matching wheels.

1929

America's car industry was booming, with flashy new designs and rising production numbers. But as the stock market crashed in October, the golden age of excess was about to hit a wall.

Leather (or leatherette) went on the back and top of Ford's Briggs-bodied Fordor "leatherback" sedan. Far more complex than the primitive Model T, the Model A cost more ($625 in this case) but buyers appreciated the extra refinement.

► Small rear side windows identified the Murray-bodied Ford Town Sedan; other Fordors had blank quarters.

◄ Bright colors could be had on Model As. This $670 Model A cabriolet was Ford's first true convertible since the Model T Coupelet. External trunks were a popular add-on.

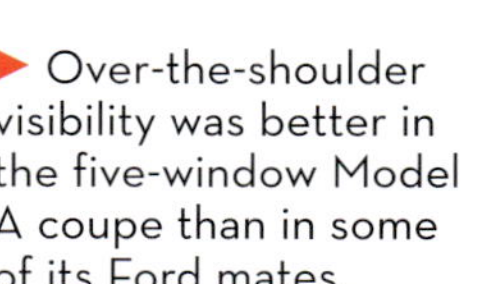

► Over-the-shoulder visibility was better in the five-window Model A coupe than in some of its Ford mates.

A 322-cid, L-head straight-eight engine powered this '29 Graham-Paige Model 827 rumb e-seat cabriolet, but the company also offered six-cylinder cars. The marque had bowed a year earlier.

This dashing 1929 Stutz Series M roadster wears a LeBaron-designed body. The 322-cid, overhead-cam straight eight worked through a four-speed gearbox.

A "Rumble Roof" gave the impression of shelter to rear occupants in a '29 Essex coupe. A graceful exit wasn't easy.

Even in sedan form, the 1929 LaSalle had graceful lines. The Series 328 line borrowed its synchromesh transmission and safety glass from upmarket big-brother Cadillac.

Note the unusual cut-down door on this 1929 Stutz M dual-cowl phaeton. Known for sport and luxury, Stutz offered an appetizing selection of bodies.

1930

Cadillac shook up the luxury market with its massive V-16 engine, the most powerful American car of its time. Meanwhile, automakers scrambled to stay afloat as the Great Depression crushed demand.

▲ The American Austin—based on its British counterpart—was built in Pennsylvania. The $465 coupe seated two and rode a short 75-inch wheelbase.

▶ Chevrolet offered one 1930 series: AD Universal. Shown is the $615 Sport Coupe; 45,311 were sold. The rear window lowered for ventilation or communication with people in the rumble seat. The 194-cid six had 50 bhp.

▼ Americans weren't ready for minicars when Austin arrived. Annual output reached 8558, then skidded. This roadster weighed in at 1100 pounds.

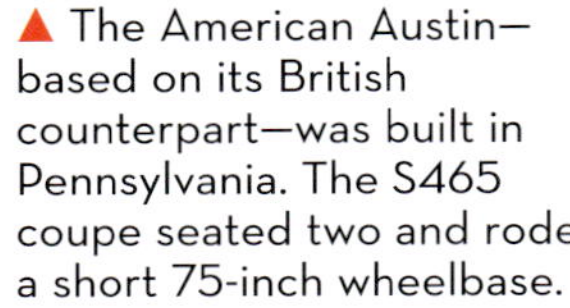

A beltline molding and lower stance minimized Buick's "pregnant" look, as on this 1930 Series 40 phaeton. Its 258-cid six developed 81 bhp. Priced at $1310, only 1100 were sold.

◀ To trounce such rivals as Packard and Peerless, Cadillac launched a V-16 for 1930. The 452-cid engine made 165 horsepower—second only to Duesenberg. Some 33 V-16 variants were listed, starting at a pricey $5350.

▼ Launched in 1929 as a '30 model, Buick's Marquette lasted only one season despite a production run of 35,007 units. It had a 67.5-bhp L-head six.

1931

Cadillac expanded its luxury lineup by offering numerous options for its prestigious V-16. At the same time, Marmon introduced the Sixteen, a sleek and powerful competitor in the V-16 market.

◀ Cadillac offered a catalog of 30 different Fleetwood-supplied bodies for its 1931 V-16, priced from $5350 to $15,000. Note the wire wheels and extra-cost wind wings on this rumble-seat roadster.

▼ Chryslers for '31 featured "Floating Power" (rubber engine mounts) and freewheeling. In addition to six-cylinder models, Chrysler offered new straight eights in four sizes.

▲ After five years of research, Marmon debuted the Sixteen. Guaranteed to do 100 mph, this coupe cost $5220. About 390 Sixteens were built between 1931 and 1933.

▼ Traction could be troublesome when driving an L-29 Cord, shown here in $2495 cabriolet form. Front-wheel drive was unproven, thus difficult to sell.

Despite the romantic aura of boattail bodies, Hudson's Greater Eight sport roadster—with 87-bhp—was built for only six months.

◀ All Buicks had straight-eight engines in 1932, including this Series 60 sedan. "Wizard Control" and "Silent Second SynchroMesh" were new features.

▼ Many consider the 1932 Confederate models, including the Sport Coupe, among the sharpest Chevys of all time. This Deluxe with sidemount tires cost $505.

▲ Cadillac's 353-cid V-8 was boosted to 115 bhp for 1932, as bodies grew more rounded. Eights sold far better than Twelves; V-16s were very rare.

▶ DeSoto launched an "All New Six" SC series in 1932, here the Custom roadster with a 75-bhp, 211.5-cid engine. A 77-bhp straight eight was also sold, but dropped after '32.

▼ A Ford Sport Coupe (*shown*) had a rumble seat; regular three-window coupes didn't. Four-cylinder cars cost $50 less than their V-8 cousins.

1932

Ford fired back with the game-changing flathead V-8, bringing affordable eight-cylinder power to the masses. Despite economic struggles, performance and style remained a priority in American car culture.

1933

Ford's 1933 models featured streamlined styling and an improved V-8. American Austin kept the dream of affordable cars alive with its fuel-efficient coupe, while Cadillac refined its V-16 with elegant new bodywork.

Dietrich supplied bodies for Packard V-12s, including the $6070 Victoria. Standard and Super Eights were also sold. Total '33 Packard output: 4803.

◀ Only three Dietrich-bodied Packard Sport Phaetons were built in 1933, on a 147-inch wheelbase, for auto shows. The rear windshield/windows folded.

▶ A vee'd grille was new to LaSalle for '33, as was GM's No-Draft Ventilation. This Series 345C RS coupe, complete with rumble seat, sold for $2245.

◀ Gracefully restyled, the '33 Ford got a more potent 75-bhp V-8 and rode a longer 112-inch wheelbase. The $510 Deluxe roadster had a rumble seat.

▲ The sparkling lines of a 1933 Auburn Salon Twelve Dual-Ratio Phaeton Sedan failed to translate into strong sales, as only 7939 Auburns were built this year.

▲ American Austin prices were cut in 1933, down to $275 for the business coupe and $315 for a roadster. Just 4726 were built, and fewer yet in '34.

▲ Fresh styling by Harley Earl gave this 1933 Cadillac V-16 Victoria skirted fenders and a unique vee'd grille, on a long 149-inch wheelbase. Note the elegant four-bar bumper.

▲ Chevrolet's two-seat roadster was gone in 1933, and its rumble-seat mate fading, as buyers turned to cabriolets. Two Chevy series were sold: a Mercury and upmarket Eagle (*shown*).

Kinship with the legendary Auburn-Cord-Duesenberg empire seems bizarre, but E. L. Cord bought Checker Taxi in 1933. A 98-bhp Lycoming straight eight powered the '33 cabs.

▶ This 1916 Chevrolet was driven to Chicago's Century of Progress, where the 1933 Chevy coach was built in a plant at the fair's GM building.

▼ Dodge dropped straight-eight engines for 1934, and never produced an Airflow. This $765 Deluxe convertible, of which 1239 were built, carried Dodge's new 87-bhp, 218-cid L-head six. This year, all Dodges were trumpted as the "New Standard."

Chrysler failed to predict public response to the shape of its radical new Airflow. This $1345 CU sedan was the most popular '34 Airflow, accounting for just over 7000 sales.

► Cadillac's 1934 restyling featured pontoon fenders, a slanted grille, and torpedo headlamps. Shown here is a $3045 355-D Eight convertible sedan.

1934

Chrysler introduced the streamlined Airflow, a revolutionary but controversial design that struggled commercially. Ford, sticking to more traditional styling, dominated sales with the Model 40.

▲ Wooden station wagons started looking a little dated by 1934. Ford (*shown*) now built its own wagon bodies, but other automakers still turned to outside suppliers.

◄ Like other GM makes, Buick adopted "Knee-Action" suspension geometry in '34. A 100-bhp, 278-cid straight eight powered this $1495 Series 60 convertible; 263 were sold.

Studebaker fielded three series in 1935: Dictator Six, Commander Eight (*shown*), and President Eight—on 114-, 120-, and 124-inch wheelbases.

1935

Dodge introduced the "New Value Six," offering style and performance at an affordable price. August Duesenberg refined the iconic Speedster with elegant updates, while Studebaker deployed three distinct series to appeal to a wide range of buyers.

▲ Not all sidemounted spares integrated this naturally. Restyled for '35, Plymouth prices now started at $510.

► Seeking a cheaper heir to the Duesenberg, Gordon Buehrig and August Duesenberg wound up creating a revived Auburn Speedster for 1935—one of the most striking Thirties machines, complete with a supercharged straight eight. At $2245, the new Auburn cost roughly half as much as an average Lincoln.

▼ Dodge named its 1935 line the "New Value Six," again with the 218-cid L-head as sole engine. Coupes came with or without a rumble seat, and 22,299 of both types were produced.

Built for the Maharajah of Indore, India, this right-drive '35 Duesenberg SJ Speedster-Roadster wore a body by J. Gurney Nutting of England.

▲ A facelift made the '36 model a prime choice of Ford fans. This $560 Deluxe roadster sold only 3862 copies; the cabriolets were far more popular.

▲ Add-on skirts added flash to a '36 Ford Deluxe Touring Sedan. With trunk, a Tudor cost $590. Horns were hidden; steel wheels replaced wires.

▲ Hupmobile trimmed its line for '36 to the 618-G Six (*shown*) and 621-N Eight, rated at 101 and 120 bhp. Hupp then closed down for 18 months.

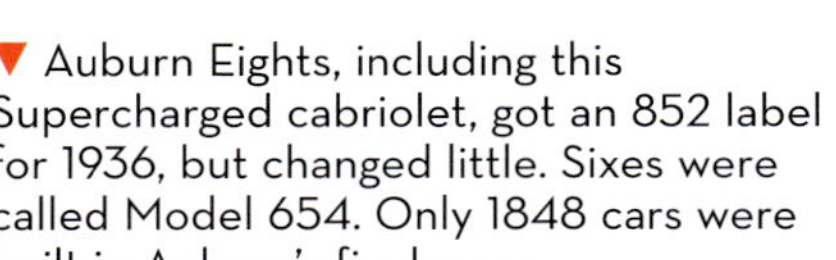

▼ Auburn Eights, including this Supercharged cabriolet, got an 852 label for 1936, but changed little. Sixes were called Model 654. Only 1848 cars were built in Auburn's final year.

1936

The Cord 810 stunned the industry thanks to its futuristic design with hidden headlights. Chevrolet's Town Sedan provided buyers with a practical, stylish option, while Ford's Deluxe Touring models offered comfort at an affordable price.

Fresh "Art Deco" styling with a tall grille gave 1936 Hudsons a slick look. Deluxe and Custom Eights (*shown*) were available, plus a Custom Six. Terraplanes sold far better.

◀ The most popular Standard '36 Chevy was the $605 Town Sedan, which sold 220,884 units. It had new hydraulic brakes and a steel roof.

▶ With a "coffin" nose and crank-up headlights, this dazzling new 1936 Cord 810 could never be mistaken for any lesser auto. A fingertip preselector activated its four-speed gearbox.

Rearward visibility wasn't a strong point of the '37 Cord 812 Custom Beverly sedan, but who cared with a body this luscious to gaze upon? Note the bustleback trunk.

1937

Ford's Tudor sedan offered a blend of affordability and modern styling, making it a popular choice among buyers of all kinds. Similarly, the 810/812 Cord showcased top-notch design and engineering.

▲ Styled by a crew under Gordon Buehrig, the 810/812 Cord was one of the top industrial designs, yet only 2320 were produced in 1936–37. Shown is the 1937 Beverly sedan.

▶ A $611 standard Ford Tudor could be formidable on police duty with the 85-bhp V-8, but economy-minded folks in '37 could choose the milder V8/60.

◀ Not many cars in 1937—or any other year—had a rear deck as long and shapely as the new $1295 Lincoln Zephyr three-passenger coupe, accentuated by rear fender skirts.

▼ Fully restyled for '37, Willys kept the old 48-bhp engine and 100-inch wheelbase. The bulged front end hinted at the forthcoming "Sharknose" Graham. Standard and Deluxe models cost $499–$589. Willys output reached 63,467.

▲ Safety glass was standard on all Chrysler products in 1937, including the restyled Plymouth P4 Deluxe. This coupe, which cost $650, attracted 67,144 new-car buyers.

▲ The 1938 Plymouth coupe didn't win many styling kudos, but America's Number Three automaker went on to produce 45,451 examples of this body style, priced from $645 to $770. A hardy 82-bhp L-head six promised reliable service.

▼ Wheelbase grew to 125 inches as part of Lincoln Zephyr's '38 restyle. Note the wind wings on this coupe.

▲ Only a handful of Pierce-Arrows went on sale in 1938, including this massive V-12 limousine. Liquidation quickly followed bankruptcy in December 1937. Pierce was best known for its fender-mounted headlights, initiated in the Teens.

Hupmobile's return to action for 1938 brought two sedan series: 822-E Six (*shown*), and the less-popular Eight.

▼ Packard offered a convertible Victoria in both the Super Eight and Twelve series (*shown*) for 1938.

1938

Plymouth's 1938 Coupe combined streamlined styling with reliable performance, making it a strong competitor in the market. This year's Willys lineup provided affordable, lightweight models.

◀ The '38 Willys lineup included new two-door sedans, plus coupes (here a $574 Deluxe) and four-door sedans. Output fell from 63,476 units to 26,691.

1939

Chevrolet's Master Deluxe Town Sedan offered buyers a refined, comfortable ride with enhanced styling. Buick continued to bridge the gap between luxury and affordability.

◀ The Hayes company built bodies for this rakish limited-edition, thin-pillared Dodge Town Coupe, well-equipped for $1055. Only 363 were produced.

▼ This top-line Master Deluxe Town Sedan with trunk was Chevrolet's bestseller in 1939: 220,181 units were sold.

Buick received a mild but pleasant facelift for 1939, with optional hidden running boards. A rumble seat was no longer offered for this $1077 Special convertible.

▼ Radio/refrigerator tycoon Powel Crosley, Jr., developed a minicar bearing his name. The 1939 Crosley had an 80-inch wheelbase and an air-cooled two-cylinder engine. Early convertible coupes and sedans were sold in hardware stores.

THE NEW 1939 "Thrifty Sixty" FORD V·8

◀ Since 1937, Ford offered two V-8s: "Thrifty Sixty" with 60 or 85 bhp. Only three 1939 Series models were available with the small V-8: coupe, Tudor, and Fordor.

A "Combination" coupe (*shown*) and two-door sedan—both $940 ($1070 Supercharged)—joined the "Sharknose" Graham line for 1939. But sales continued to languish: just 5392 units.

▲ Running boards were a $10 option on the Dodge Deluxe sedan, which had a starting price of $905. 84,976 were built.

▼ Modern profiles on longer wheelbases marked the 1940 Chrysler line, like this $960 six-cylinder Royal coupe.

No ordinary 1940 Cadillac, this dazzling convertible wears a custom body, with neatly dipped-down doors by Bohman & Schwartz. Built on a Series Sixty-Two chassis with the stock 135-bhp, 346-cid V-8, this car even sports bucket seats.

1940

Buick and Cadillac rolled out powerful straight-eight engines, bringing more refinement to the mid-range and luxury markets. Dodge's Deluxe Sedan provided a spacious and reliable option.

▼ Glamour in Packard's 1940 lineup came from custom-built Darrins, styled by Howard "Dutch" Darrin. This is the $4593 Super Eight One Eighty Victoria.

▲ Buicks came in six series for 1940. Special, Super, Century, Road Master, Limited 80, and top-of-the-line Limited 90. Only 550 copies of this $1343 Century convertible were built. This was the last year for the sidemounted spare tire.

1941

With war on the horizon and the Great Depression in the rear view, the market grew—as total industry production came to be 3,744,300 cars and 1,094,261 trucks.

▼ Nash turned to unit construction in 1941 for the new, smaller "600" series, but not for the big Ambassador, here a fastback sedan. The Ambassador six delivered 105 bhp; the eight, 115 bhp.

▼ The top-priced Packard series for 1941 was the One Eighty, including this $4695 Custom Super Eight All-Weather Cabriolet by Rollson.

▲ Only 2045 Chevrolet Special Deluxe station wagons were built in 1941—a price topper at $995. Lots of extras could be ordered, from vacuum shift to turn signals to bumper guards.

▼ Cars don't get much prettier than this '41 Cadillac Series Sixty-Two convertible sedan, benefiting from a major styling update. Only 400 of these $1965 ragtops were produced. A new Series Sixty-One replaced the departed LaSalle.

Willys called its slightly enlarged 1941 models "Americar." In Speedway, DeLuxe, and Plainsman trim, each had a 63-bhp, 134-cid four.

▲ Graham halted production of the Cord-based Custom Hollywood sedan in September 1940, but a fair number of remaining cars were sold as '41s.

◀ Unlike most '41s, Plymouth clung to running boards. This $1007 Special Deluxe convertible showed off the facelift; 10,545 were sold.

▼ Most convertibles were still without rear side windows in 1941. Pontiac's handsome $1048 Deluxe Torpedo Eight was no exception to the rule.

▲ Studebaker bored the Champion six to 167 cid, getting 80 bhp for '41. Note the two-toning on this $860 Champion DeLux-Tone Cruising Sedan.

▶ Convertible phaetons still existed in Buick's 1941 Super and Roadmaster series. At $1555 and $1775, sales reached only 508 and 326 units, respectively.

▶ Introduced a year earlier, Chrysler's steel-roofed 1942 Town & Country was unlike any other "woody" wagon—and was the first such model offered by the company. A sloping rear roof and "clamshell" doors gave the original Chrysler Town & Country a unique spot in wagon history.

▲ Stylists drew from GM's "Y-Job" show car when reworking '42 Buicks. Sweeping full-length "Airfoil" fenders graced most models, including this Roadmaster convertible.

▼ Could this 1942 Hudson Commodore Eight sedan be aspiring to official duty with that red spotlight?

▼ DeSoto convertible coupes came in DeLuxe and Custom trim in 1942. A plush Custom Town Sedan, dubbed Fifth Avenue, featured leather and Bedford cloth upholstery trim. Only DeSoto presented a dramatically different face for 1942, in the form of hidden "airfoil" headlights, billed as "out of sight except at night." A larger six made 115 bhp.

▲ Just 1185 Dodge Custom convertibles were built in the brief model year, with a larger (230-cid) 105-bhp six.

◀ Two-tone paint looked fine on a 1942 Chevrolet Fleetline Aerosedan. This body style had been popular in other GM divisions in 1941, and sold well in the short '42 season. Chevrolet claimed the title "America's Most Popular Car." The new Fleetline subseries included a "torpedo-style" Aerosedan and conventional Sportmaster four door.

1942

Automakers halted civilian production as the U.S. entered World War II, converting factories to build tanks, planes, and military vehicles. The last new American cars rolled off the line in February before the industry went full war mode.

1943

The war effort pressed on. As car manufacturers remained focused on military production, Americans continued to drive 1942 models.

◀ The Lincoln Continental's V-12 engine earned a 1942 enlargement to 305 inches, for 10 extra horsepower. Only 200 club coupes were produced, with a $3000 price tag. Facelifting of the 1942 Lincoln Continental roughly foretold its postwar look. Fenders were taller and longer, with headlamps flanked by dual parking lights.

▶ Still sitting in the shadow of the classic Continental, Lincoln's Zephyr earned a similar restyling for the abbreviated 1942 season. Note the pushbutton-operated doors on this $2150 convertible, like those on the Continental. A three-passenger coupe, club coupe, and four-door sedan also made the 1942 lineup. The last prewar Lincoln left the factory on February 10, 1942, after a run of just 6547 cars.

▼ A spotlight wasn't standard fare on a 1942 Mercury convertible coupe. Like other makes, "blackout" Mercurys produced after December 1941 had painted, not chromed, trim.

Mercury's flathead V-8 engine got a boost from 95 to 100 bhp for 1942. A semiautomatic "Liquamatic" transmission could be ordered—but soon proved troublesome.

▶ Packard unveiled the trendsetting Clipper in mid 1941, positioned between the One Twenty and One Sixty. Both "Dutch" Darrin and Packard's stylists contributed to the modern design, which featured a slim grille and a flush-sided "envelope" body, wider than it was tall.

▼ Packard's own designers penned this upright '42 One Eighty limousine, far removed from the pending "Clipper" shape.

▲ Just 31,780 Nashes were made before the government-ordered closing. The last of the line were "blackout" models.

◀ A Nash Ambassador rode a 121-inch wheelbase and could be powered by either a six- or eight-cylinder engine.

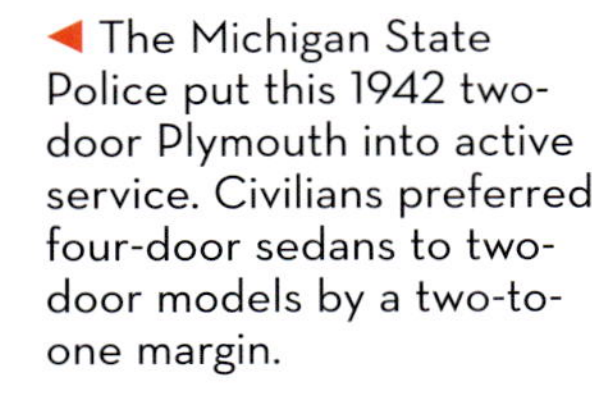

◀ The Michigan State Police put this 1942 two-door Plymouth into active service. Civilians preferred four-door sedans to two-door models by a two-to-one margin.

▼ Pontiac explained that the '42 model looked much wider, despite modest growth overall. Reasons: a broader grille, hood, and bumpers, with headlamps spaced farther apart.

▶ Final prewar Plymouths, like other Detroit cars, had "blackout" trim to save on materials for the war effort.

1944

Car manufacturers, now experts in mass production for military needs, prepared to return to civilian manufacturing postwar. Meanwhile, demand for personal vehicles built up, setting the stage for a postwar boom.

▼ Pontiac's 1942 line included Streamliner and Torpedo (*shown*), each available with a six or eight.

1945

As World War II ended, American automakers scrambled to restart production. The first postwar cars were essentially warmed-over prewar designs, but big changes were coming.

▶ General Motors produced 854,000 trucks for wartime use, including these near-ready light-duty models.

◀ Two-thirds of the heavy trucks employed during World War II came from GM plants.

Developed by the GMC Truck & Coach Division, the amphibious "Duck" saw duty worldwide during World War II, carrying troops on land or water. All five GM passenger-car divisions also turned their facilities over to the war effort. Many M-24 light tanks used Cadillac V-8 engines and Hydra-Matic transmissions.

▼ The star on the door marks this 1942 Packard sedan as a military staff car.

▲ Henry Ford II drives the first civilian postwar Ford off the assembly line on July 3, 1945. Production resumed just after V-J (Victory in Japan) Day.

1946

Car production restarted using prewar designs. Demand for new vehicles surged as soldiers returned home.

Only one Ford was new for 1946: the $1982 wood-trimmed Super DeLuxe Sportsman.

◀ Cadillac's Series Sixty-Two sedanet (also called a club coupe) was no lightweight at 4145 pounds.

▼ The 1946 Ford "coupe sedan" came only in top Super DeLuxe trim. Price: $1307 with a V-8.

▲ Because the wood-trimmed Town & Country was Chrysler's glamour car, celebrities were engaged to hawk its virtues. Here, singer Marie McDonald shows off a convertible.

▼ Headlights were no longer hidden on the postwar DeSotos. This 1946 Custom convertible went for $1761.

Two of these 1946 Chrysler "Continental" coupes were specially built. Both went to the same man, who liked the look of the Lincoln Continental. Priced at $17,000 apiece, the cars had squared-off, top-opening trunks with exposed spare tires, and padded leatherette tops. The coupes rode on a Saratoga chassis and carried 135-bhp eights. From B-posts forward, they looked all-Chrysler.

► Except for a new cross-hatch grille, the 1946 Dodge Custom convertible was similar to its prewar counterpart. Its 102-bhp six now started with a dashboard button.

◄ Plymouths took DeLuxe or Special DeLuxe form for '46, with the same 95-bhp, 217.8-cid six as in 1942. Utility models were deleted from the line.

▼ ► A total of 5690 two-door (*below*) and four-door (*right*) sedans were produced in Packard's posh Custom Super Clipper series. Interiors featured broadcloth or leather upholstery. Packard offered no convertibles or station wagon models.

Pontiacs wore a simplified grille for 1947, when a six-cylinder Torpedo convertible sold for $1811 ($1853 in DeLuxe trim). Eights added $43 to the price.

◄ Idaho troopers didn't have to endure spartan patrol duty while driving this Fleetline Aerosedan—the most-costly two-door Chevrolet sedan, and also the most popular.

1947

Automakers introduced minor updates to prewar models. The industry prepared for fresh postwar designs.

"Dramatic" barely describes the 1947 Studebaker, styled by Virgil Exner and Robert Bourke.

1948

Cadillac introduced the first tailfins, kicking off a new styling trend. Tucker debuted its short-lived but innovative sedan.

► Kaiser-Frazer touted 35 improvements in style and mechanical details for 1948. In reality, this $2746 Frazer Manhattan didn't look much different from the '47, though its price rose moderately. Posh interiors helped the Manhattan attract customers, but a standard Frazer was a less-expensive alternative.

▼ Spotlights weren't part of the $1857 price of a 1948 Plymouth Special DeLuxe convertible, which had no rear side windows.

Tuckers were roomy, powerful, and aerodynamic. The rear-mounted flat-six engine delivered 166 bhp and a walloping 372 pound-feet of torque.

▲ Despite the growth of suburbia, the era of wood-bodied wagons was ending. This 1948 Super DeLuxe Ford seated eight, and 8912 were built.

▼ Modestly sized when they first appeared on the 1948 Cadillac, tailfins would soon grow enormous. This Series Sixty-One sedanet, at $2728, was Cadillac's cheapest model.

▲ Carrying a 94-bhp, 226-cid six, the Studebaker Commander Regal DeLuxe convertible cost $2431.

▼ "Tip-toe" shift cost $121 extra on DeSotos. Shown is a 1948 Custom convertible, priced at $2296.

▲ Last examples of the classic Lincoln Continental came off the line in 1948. Henry Ford II drove a convertible to pace the Indianapolis 500 this year.

◀ Driving the $1765 Jeepster was the same engine that had powered prewar Americars: a 134-cid four, rated at 63 bhp. First-year output topped 10,000.

▶ The 1948 Oldsmobile "Futuramic" 98, from Harley Earl's Art & Colour studio, was one of GM's first totally new postwar designs.

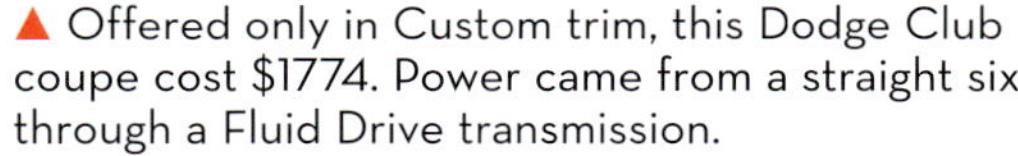

▲ Offered only in Custom trim, this Dodge Club coupe cost $1774. Power came from a straight six through a Fluid Drive transmission.

▲ Fleetline fastbacks wore Chevy's 1949 restyling well. A DeLuxe four-door cost $1539. More than 130,323 were built.

▼ Buick—along with fellow GM makes Cadillac and Olds—pioneered the hardtop convertible with the '49 Roadmaster Riviera. At $3203, it cost $53 more than the soft top; 4343 were built.

◀ Crosley took a shot at sports-car fans with the new doorless $849 Hotshot, which surprised many people with its racing prowess. Only 752 '49s were built.

▼ Lincoln offered junior and senior ragtops for '49. This "Junior" standard model listed at $3116.

Pontiac's "Silver Streak" hood trim was bolder than ever for '49. This DeLuxe Chieftain Eight listed at $1924.

The elegant standard Sport Sedan was Lincoln's best-seller. Total Lincoln output was 73,507 units.

1949

Buick's Roadmaster Riviera introduced a stylish, fastback design that set a new standard for postwar luxury cars. Pontiac's DeLuxe Chieftain Eight offered a smooth ride with an upgraded V-8 engine and signature hood trim.

 100 YEARS OF AMERICAN CARS

1950

Automatic transmissions gained popularity. Car culture grew with well-formed styling and classic elegance.

◀ Plymouth dechromed for 1950—and looked better for it. The convertible was sold only in Special Deluxe trim.

▼ Buick again listed long-chassis Super and Roadmaster Riviera sedans for '51, here the $3044 Roadmaster; 48,758 were produced.

Like all 1950 Buicks, the Roadmaster Riviera hardtop wore more-shapely styling and higher prices. This new Deluxe-trim version listed for $2854.

▲ Nash's Rambler bowed as a convertible in March 1950, followed by a two-door wagon in June. It would quickly prove to be America's most successful postwar compact.

▼ Oldsmobile's little-changed 88 convertible remained fast, flashy, and highly desirable in 1950—and 9127 were sold.

Lincoln still lacked hardtops for '51, so the stand-in Cosmopolitan Capri coupe returned at $3350 with a wider "mouth" and reshuffled trim.

▼ Lido, which remained Lincoln's standard-series pseudo-hardtop for '51, measured 214.8 inches overall.

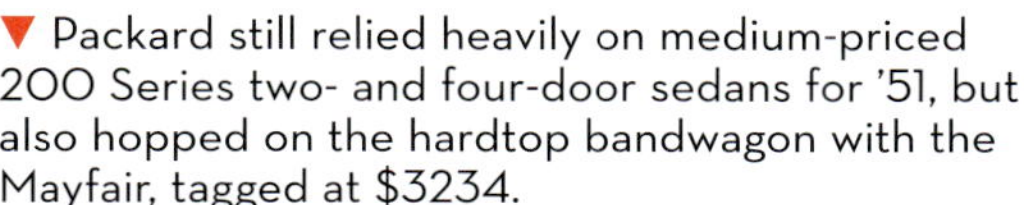

▼ Packard still relied heavily on medium-priced 200 Series two- and four-door sedans for '51, but also hopped on the hardtop bandwagon with the Mayfair, tagged at $3234.

▲ Unlike the '51 Mercurys and standard Lincolns, which wore newly extended rear fenders, Lincoln Cosmopolitans retained a rounded look—plus top-shelf trim and equipment, of course. List price was $3891, a lofty sum at the time.

▲ Chrysler's new "Firepower" 180-bhp V-8 won Indy official pace car honors for the New Yorker ragtop.

▼ Ford's Crestliner returned for '51 at $1595 (a $116 price cut!). But after only 8073 were built it was dropped.

1951

Chrysler introduced its "Firepower" V-8 engine, providing augmented levels of power and performance. Ford's Crestliner featured sleek styling and a smooth ride.

1952

Ford's Sunliner offered a stylish convertible option with a smoother ride, perfect for leisurely drives. Hudson's Hornet Club Coupe combined performance with elegance.

▼ A look inside the '52 Aero Willys shows uncommon roominess for a compact, and simple, functional trim.

Glamour leader of Ford's '52 line was the new Sunliner convertible, priced at $2027; 22,534 were built.

Willys returned to passenger cars for '52 with the Aero Willys. Among the three two-door models offered was this $1989 Aero-Wing; 12,819 copies were sold.

▲ Hudson's "Step-down" design, now in its fifth season, was starting to look dated when this Hornet Club Coupe was built.

▼ Plymouth's first hardtop bowed for '51 as the $2114 Cranbrook Belvedere. This nearly identical '52 model added the distinctive "saddleback" two-tone treatment.

Ford was all-new for 1952, thus more competitive against holdover Chevy and Plymouth—but Korean War-related conservation forced production cutbacks.

▼ The Chrysler Special show car was built by coachbuilder Ghia of Italy, but designed by Highland Park's Virgil Exner. It was one of several "idea cars" used to jazz up Chrysler's image during a period of dull production styling.

◀ Buick's '52 Special line again used Chevy/Pontiac tooling. Exclusive to the series was this $2115 "Tourback" two-door sedan; only 2206 were built.

▲ Pontiac offered a sedan delivery in the early '50s, but sales were slim—only 984 units for '52. The famous "Silver Streak" trim is evident on this example.

▲ The Pontiac line sported a new look for 1953. This well-chromed Chieftain Eight Catalina hardtop sold for $2446.

▼ This '53 Mercury Monterey played a part in Ford Motor Company's 50th anniversary hoopla. Posing (*from left to right*) are Ford brothers Henry II, Benson, and William Clay.

1953

Pontiac's Chieftain Eight Catalina combined striking design with solid performance. Buick introduced its new ohv "Fireball" V-8, which featured both better performance and efficiency.

▲ This '53 Crestline Sunliner did official pace car duty at that year's Indianapolis 500, honoring Ford's 50th anniversary.

◀ The $3002 Super boasted vastly improved performance over predecessors with Buick's new ohv "Fireball" V-8.

▼ Though denied the new ohv V-8, the $2197 Special four-door remained Buick's most-popular car for 1953, selling 100,312 units.

1954

Ford's Crestline Skyliner featured a distinctive "glass top," which gave it its unique touch. Chevrolet's Corvette became an iconic car that captured the eyes of many thanks to its breathtaking design and powerful performance.

▶ This 1954 Nash Statesman Custom Country Club hardtop is a rarity (2726 were built). It sold new for $2423.

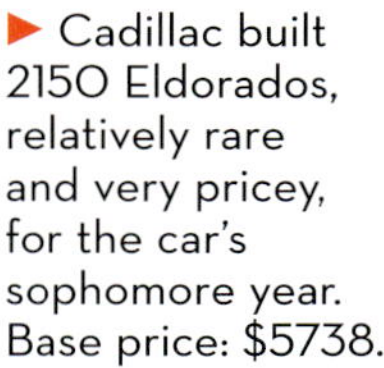

▶ Cadillac built 2150 Eldorados, relatively rare and very pricey, for the car's sophomore year. Base price: $5738.

▼ Though little-changed from its introduction, Chevy's Corvette saw 1954 output jump to 3640.

▲▼ Ford's new '54 Crestline Skyliner sported a green-tint Plexiglas front half-roof that brought the outside inside—and, according to critics, made people perspire on sunny days.

GM show-car styling arrived on the '54 Buicks. Here, the $2964 Super.

▲ Chevy's first V-8 since 1917 bowed for 1955 with 265 cubic inches and 162 or 180 horsepower.

▼ The Series Sixty-Two four-door sedan remained Cadillac's best-selling model for banner 1955: 45,300 units.

1955

The Chevrolet Bel Air became an instant classic. V-8 engines and bold styling defined the decade's mid-point.

◀ A modern new 287 V-8 was standard across a smaller, but more focused, '55 Pontiac line. Here is the Star Chief Custom Catalina hardtop, priced at $2499.

▼ Chevy's new '55 Bel Air Nomad pioneered the "hardtop" wagon, but attracted just 8386 buyers.

Distinctive "shark" fins graced Cadillac's '55 Eldorado, and would do so for several years. Price was up sharply to $6286, and so were sales.

▲ Once Buick's best-seller, the next-to-the-top Super line again included this $2831 Riviera hardtop coupe.

▼ Only 4243 Buick Century Estate Wagons were built for 1955. The hefty $3175 base price may have held down sales.

Buicks were occasionally chosen for police work, as was the relatively light Century two-door sedan shown here.

▼ Lincoln was one of Detroit's few '55s without a trendy wraparound windshield. This Capri hardtop sold new for $3910, and 11,462 were built.

◀ Every '55 Chevy was all-new, but none were more desirable than the $2305 Bel Air V-8 convertible.

◀ Cadillac's own 1955 Series Sixty-Two convertible wore a tasteful facelift of its all-new '54 styling. List price: $4448.

▲ Stylist Dick Teague conjured a remarkable '55 facelift that made Packard's '51 bodyshell look almost new. The Caribbean ragtop again topped the line, at $5932.

1956

Seat belts started appearing in some models. Cars grew larger, flashier, and more powerful.

Chevrolet joined the movement to four-door hardtops for 1956 with the pillarless Sport Sedans.

▶ Like sister MoPar makes, Dodge sported prominent tailfins for 1956, as on this $2513 V-8 Royal sedan.

▼ A big new 368-cubic-inch V-8 with 285 horses powered all '56 Lincolns, like this $4601 Premiere sedan.

▼ A new, smaller ultraluxury Caddy made its debut for '57 as the Eldorado Brougham, a show-car-inspired hardtop shockingly priced at $13,074.

▲ Chevrolet's Corvette was all-new and dramatically improved for 1956. A new lift-off hardtop option shown here helped boost model-year output to 3467.

▲ Chrysler's 1956 Windsors wore their own unique grille for the first—and last—time. This four-door sedan was the line's best-selling model with 53,119 orders.

▲ Chevy crafted the lightweight Corvette Sebring Special to win the 12-hour Florida race in 1957. It was fast—but unfortunately failed to finish.

◀ Production Corvettes changed little on the surface, but available fuel injection boosted horsepower to 283.

▼ Thunderbird was handsomely restyled for '57, the last year for the original two-seater. Exactly 21,380 were built.

The ultraluxury Continental Mark II returned for 1957 with 15 additional horsepower—300 total—as the only significant change.

▲ At about $2500, the Ford Country Sedan (186,889 built) seated six or eight folks.

◀ Cadillac rebodied 1957, nicely blending boxy and rounded lines on the Eldorado Biarritz, whose price was up to a staggering $7286.

1957

Cadillac's Eldorado Biarritz set the standard for luxury with its stunning design and V-8 engine. The Ford Thunderbird's restyling further proved why it's an iconic American car.

▶ For 1958, Olds again offered a convertible in all three of its series. This midrange Super 88 version cost $3529 and attracted 3799 customers.

▼ All-new styling dressed the 1958 Chevys (*bottom*) and the Corvette (*middle*). Providing a glimpse of the future, the experimental Biscayne (*top*) and Sebring SS (*far right*).

1958

Tailfins reached their peak as cars got bigger and heavier. The economy slowed, affecting auto sales.

A pair of Lincoln-Mercury executives try out a Mark III convertible in this 1958 factory press photo taken at Ford's Dearborn Proving Grounds.

▼ Three bare-bones Scotsman models were Stude's best-sellers—20,872 units—though this $1795 two-door sedan chalked up just 5538 sales.

▲ Bonneville was Pontiac's top-line model for 1958. This $3481 hardtop coupe was new to the line. Fender script here identifies optional fuel injection with 310 horsepower.

▼ Ford president Henry Ford II chauffeurs brothers Benson and William Clay in this publicity shot staged to launch the new 1958 Edsel. This top-line Citation ragtop cost $3801.

1959

Mercury's Park Lane offered a blend of luxury and performance with its bold styling and powerful engine options. Chrysler's 1959 lineup featured ordinary styling and more of what's been seen before.

▲ Pretty in pink or burgundy, Ford's '59 Thunderbird weighed 3903 pounds and attracted 10,261 buyers.

▼ Chevy's Corvette output rose by roughly 500, to a healthier 9670 units. Curb weight was 2840 pounds.

▲ Pontiac soared to fourth in industry sales with its all-new "Wide-Track" '59 models. This $3478 Bonneville convertible attracted 11,426 sun worshippers.

▶ Mercury's 1959s were fairly tasteful despite newly added bulk. At $4206, this Park Lane convertible was the priciest model. Only 1257 were built.

Olds continued offering three ragtops for 1959, with the Dynamic 88 the most affordable at $3286. Here is one of 8491 examples built during the model run.

▲ A rather uninspired facelift marked 1959's "Lion-Hearted" Chryslers. Windsors like this $3289 hardtop coupe used a new 305-horse V-8.

▲ The 1959 Chryslers gained more than 6000 sales over the '58s, but the $4890 New Yorker convertible dropped from 666 to a mere 286.

▲ Chrysler's 1959 300-E kept the big trapezoid grille from 1957–58 and looked better for it. The $5319 hardtop weighed 4290 pounds.

A part of the 1959 Ford Fairlane 500 Galaxie family, the Skyliner managed 12,915 sales—too few to be continued.

▲ The rarest of post-1954 Imperials are the special Ghia-built Crown Imperial limousines. This is one of only seven built to 1959 specs. Cost: $15,075.

► Invicta replaced the Century as Buick's midrange series for '59. Among its five models was this hardtop sedan priced at $3515.

▶ Fins flew high on the all-new 1960 "Unibody" Chrysler lineup. The $4875 New Yorker convertible (*right*) snared only 556 buyers.

▼ Oldsmobile traded 1959's "Linear Look" for cleaner "Balanced Design" on its 1960 models, shown here by a pair of Ninety Eight hardtops. Prices: $4086 and $4162.

▼ This $3663 hardtop coupe was one of six models available in DeSoto's 1960 Adventurer lineup.

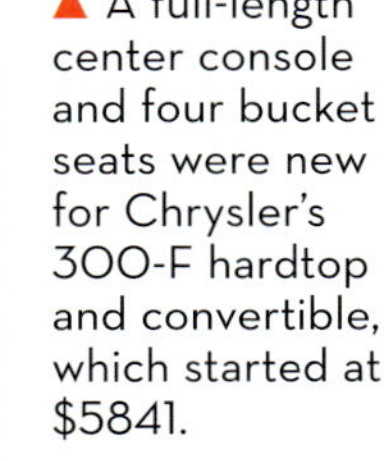

1960

Chrysler introduced its "Unibody" lineup, which had many structural improvements. Similarly, DeSoto's Adventurer lineup combined power and comfort to capture the interest of many.

▲ A number of design tweaks—and up to 315 fuel-injected horses—made Chevy's 1960 Corvette the best yet. Sales finally broke the 10,000 mark.

▲ A full-length center console and four bucket seats were new for Chrysler's 300-F hardtop and convertible, which started at $5841.

◀ A more conventional face appeared on all full-size 1960 Chevrolets, including the popular Impala Sport Coupe hardtop. It sold for $2599 with the standard 135-horse six.

1961

The Lincoln Continental introduced rear-hinged "suicide doors." Performance and luxury became key selling points.

▶ Lincoln lost many pounds, inches, and models with 1961's all-new Continental. This revived convertible sedan, of which only 2857 were built, retailed for a lofty $6713. Wheelbase was now 123 inches, down by eight.

▼ Plymouth's 1961 full-size sales fell sharply. The $2967 Fury V-8 convertible appealed to just 6948 customers.

▶ Mercury's compact Comet came back for '61 with modest changes, but a new bucket-seat S-22 coupe was the big news. Here, the standard two-door, which listed at an even $2000.

▼ Dart remained Dodge's mainstay seller for '61, when a heavy facelift made it look more like senior models. Seen here is the top-line Phoenix hardtop coupe.

▲ Studebaker's Lark compacts were lightly facelifted for '61, and sales slipped. Here, the top-line Regal convertible; 1981 were produced. This Lark weighed 3315 pounds.

◀ Oldsmobile helped start the swing to sporty big cars with the new mid-1961 Starfire, a specially trimmed Super 88 convertible priced at $4647. Just 7600 found buyers.

Buick revived its familiar Special name for new 1961 compacts with crisp lines, small all-aluminum V-8, and standard or Deluxe trim.

▼ Dart wagons in 1961 consisted of Seneca and Pioneer models, the latter with room for six or nine. Wagon prices ranged from $2695 to $3011.

▼ A flexible "rope" driveshaft and rear transaxle made Pontiac's Tempest the most radical of General Motors's new "second wave" '61 compacts.

▲ The 1961 Bonneville Sport Coupe revived 1959's split-theme grille. All of the "Bonnies" rode a 123-inch chassis.

▲ Valiants changed little for 1961, but again sold well—143,078 units—though they couldn't entirely offset Plymouth's big-car losses. This V200 wagon listed at $2423.

◀ Tempest bowed with four-door sedans and wagons, adding coupes at midyear. All offered base or Custom trim.

▲ Designer Brooks Stevens gave 1962 Studebaker Larks a Mercedes-look grille and a $185 Skytop fabric sunroof, as on this $2190 Regal four-door. Unfortunately, sales kept sliding.

◀ Sales of AMC's mini Metropolitan reached 412 for '62, though assembly had actually ceased in mid 1960.

▼ Unlike the Bel Air, Chevy's 1962 Impala hardtop coupe (*SS shown*) wore a new, more "formal" roofline.

▲ Buick broadened the appeal of its compact Special for 1962 with convertibles in Deluxe and, shown here, bucket-seat Skylark trim. At $3012, it attracted 8913 buyers. The $2879 Deluxe sold 8332 copies.

1962

Buick's Skylark offered compact and stylish options, while Plymouth's Signet appealed to the growing demand for affordable luxury.

▲ The '61 Plymouth Valiant V200 hardtop gained bucket seats to become the 1962 Signet. Priced at $2230, it garnered 25,586 sales. The "Slant Six" again gave 101 or 145 optional horses.

◀ The "ducktail" Corvette returned for '62 with even tidier looks (no two-toning), plus enlarged V-8s with up to 360 horses. Base price was also up, to $4038, but so were sales, to a record 14,531 units.

1963

The Chevrolet Corvette Sting Ray coupe introduced a bold new design, cementing it as an American icon. Dodge's Polara provided a mix of performance and style.

▲ The 1963 model would be the only Sting Ray coupe with the unique "split" rear window. The coupe weighed in at a lean 2859 pounds.

▲ Nonletter Chrysler 300s paced the 1963 Indy 500, and a replica "Pace Setter" convertible (*shown*) and hardtop coupe were issued. Ragtop orders totaled 1861 units.

▲ Styling for the 1963 Dodge Polara was toned down. Hardtops like this one found 6823 buyers. Prices started at $2965.

▲ Chrysler launched a consumer test program of its latest automotive gas-turbine engine in 1963. The engine was packaged in this striking hardtop coupe styled by Elwood Engel. Fifty cars were built by Ghia in Italy.

Imperial lost its "gunsight" taillamps for '63. This is the $5243 Custom hardtop; 3264 were built.

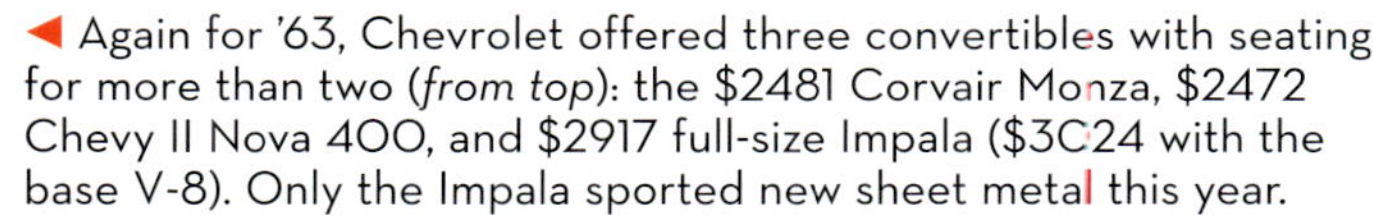

◀ Again for '63, Chevrolet offered three convertibles with seating for more than two (*from top*): the $2481 Corvair Monza, $2472 Chevy II Nova 400, and $2917 full-size Impala ($3024 with the base V-8). Only the Impala sported new sheet metal this year.

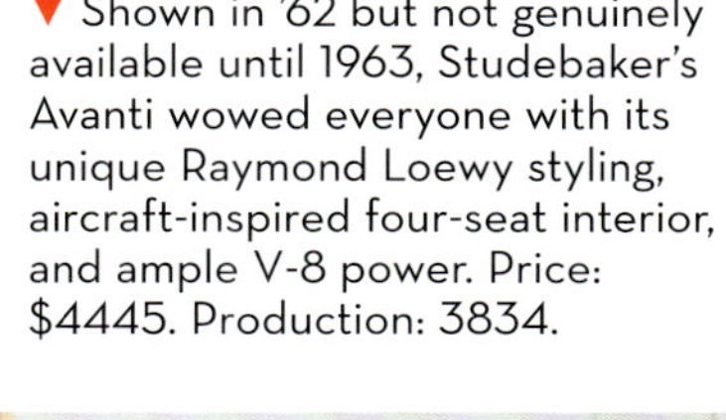

▼ Shown in '62 but not genuinely available until 1963, Studebaker's Avanti wowed everyone with its unique Raymond Loewy styling, aircraft-inspired four-seat interior, and ample V-8 power. Price: $4445. Production: 3834.

▲ Obviously ready for quarter-mile action, this two-door '64 Dodge 330 is a rare "Hemi-Charger" with the factory Maximum Performance Package.

▼ The 1964 Studebakers, here the $2805 Daytona ragtop, would be the last to be built in South Bend, Indiana.

1964

Ford launched the Mustang, creating the ponycar segment. 1964 Daytona ragtops closed production in Indiana.

AMC's small 1964 Rambler Americans wore attractive all-new styling on a six-inch-longer wheelbase (106 inches). Here, the top-trim 440 convertible, hardtop, and wagon.

► Buicks looked brawnier for '64. Sporty Wildcats, like this $3267 hardtop coupe, boasted a new 425-inch V-8 option with either 340 or 360 horsepower.

▲ The full-size "Jet Smooth" Chevrolets looked a little boxier for 1964. Impala SS was again the sportiest of the lot, though this tamer hardtop coupe came with a 140-horse six for $2839.

▼ Mercury marked its Silver Anniversary in 1964 with a facelifted full-size line led by performance-oriented Marauder semifastback hardtops like this Montclair.

The Rambler Classic Typhoon hardtop bowed in mid 1964 to introduce a modern new inline six of the same name (232 inch, 145 horse). Just 2520 were sold at $2509 apiece.

▼ Ford opened up a big new market with the Falcon-based Mustang. Introduced on April 17, 1964, as a '65 model, the new sporty compact sent people scurrying to Ford showrooms like nothing in years, touching off "Mustang Mania" and Detroit's greatest sales success of the Sixties. This ragtop cost $2614 with the 101-horsepower six, and scored an amazing (for a ragtop) 101,945 sales.

▼ Atypical for Detroit, Chevy's stunning Corvette Sting Ray returned for 1964 with less "gingerbread," which on fastbacks like this also meant a one-piece instead of a split rear window. Base price was still $4252; 8304 were built.

▶ Studebaker's Avanti returned for 1964 with a $4445 price tag and square headlamp bezels as one of the few changes from debut '63. A 240-horse 289-inch V-8 remained standard, and options ran to a 290-horse "R2" version—or a 335-horse, 305-inch "R3." Unfortunately, sales dropped from 3834 to just 809, which helped force Studebaker's exit from South Bend.

1965

The Mustang continued to have success, and the late 1960s would see numerous competitors enter the market.

This racy "2+2" fastback expanded the Mustang stable for the 1965 model year, and galloped off with 77,079 buyers.

◀ The Corvair Greenbrier wagon was in its final year for '65.Just 1528 were sold this year at $2609 apiece.

▼ Dodge built only a few '65 Hemi-Coronet "altereds" for drag racing. Like "Dandy" Dick Landy's mount here, they were banned by NHRA and thus ran only in AHRA.

▼ American Motors tried to one-up Ford's Mustang 2+2 fastback with its mid-1965 Marlin. Priced at $3100 with the 232-cubic-inch six, it offered a wide range of options and attracted 10,327 customers.

Widely advertised as being "Quiet as a Rolls-Royce," the Galaxie 500 LTD was the costliest and cushiest of the all-new 1965 full-size Fords. This hardtop sedan stickered at $3313, and notched an impressive 68,038 sales.

◀ First seen in 1964, the mid-engine Ford GT40 endurance racer won the grueling Le Mans 24 Hours in 1966 in this Ferrari-eater "Mark II" guise. In addition, a few roadgoing cars were later built as "Mark III" models.

Lincoln's 1966 redo added five inches of length, plus a massive 462-cubic-inch V-8. A new hardtop coupe, priced at $5485, helped boost Lincoln build to 54,755.

After record sales in 1965, Cadillac stood basically pat for '66, yet fared nearly as well. Here, the $5555 De Ville convertible, whose sales held steady at just over 19,000.

▲ Ford asked Carroll Shelby, creator of the awesome early Sixties Cobra sports cars, to turn Mustangs into race winners. His answer, the '65 GT-350, saw few changes for '66. Price: $4557.

1966

The Ford GT40 made a major impact on the racing world. Chevrolet's Caprice introduced both wagon and two-door options.

▲ The Ford Thunderbird completed another three-year styling cycle for 1966 with a new pointy nose and eggcrate grille, plus wall-to-wall taillights. The soft top, shown here, stickered at $4879, but sales were down to just 5049 units. Because Thunderbird ragtop sales continued to fall, the body style would not return for '67. A 390-inch V-8, upped to 315 bhp, was still standard.

Built on a new B-body platform shared with the Plymouth Belvedere/Satellite, the '66 Dodge Coronets wore crisp, fairly conservative lines. Here, the 500 convertible (*shown*), which sold for $2600–$2900. Including the four-door sedan, 55,683 Coronet 500s were produced.

▲ Ambassador also became a separate AMC "make" for 1966, and offered a swank new top-line hardtop model: DPL. It started at $2756, and 10,458 were built.

▼ Midsize '66 Buicks got a "midlife" makeover. Big-inch bucket-seat Gran Sports were now a separate line distinct from Skylarks, which included a new hardtop sedan, shown here with the $3019 GS hardtop coupe, of which 9934 were built.

▲ Chevy followed up on the success of the 1965 Caprice hardtop sedan by adding wagons and this two-door with its own greenhouse for 1966. Total Caprice output: 181,000 units.

▼Chevy dropped "fuelie" small-blocks for 1966, leaving a big new 427-inch V-8 with up to 425 horses as Corvette's ultimate 1966 power option. It came with a domed hood. The $4295 coupe sold 9958 copies this year.

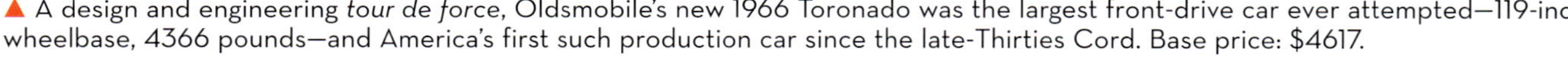

▲ A design and engineering *tour de force*, Oldsmobile's new 1966 Toronado was the largest front-drive car ever attempted—119-inch wheelbase, 4366 pounds—and America's first such production car since the late-Thirties Cord. Base price: $4617.

1967

Chevrolet introduced the Camaro to rival the Mustang. Safety regulations led to changes in car design.

▲ Though Buick built some of the most potent muscle cars of the Sixties, some models were surprisingly rare. This 1967 GS 400 convertible saw production of only 2140 units. The $3167 base price may have helped squelch demand.

▼ Trendy new "coke bottle" fenderlines and an updated chassis made the '67 Ambassador AMC's best big car yet. The top-line DPL hardtop coupe shown here cost $2958.

▶ The huge success of Ford's Mustang inspired Chevy's new-for-'67 Camaro. This $2466 hardtop coupe has the SS and RS packages, two of the many extra-cost items offered to entice buyers. Total Camaro sales for 1967: 220,917.

▲ A mild facelift marked '67 Chevy Chevelles, like this SS 396 convertible, of which only 2286 were built. This model started at $3102, $239 more than the Malibu V-8 ragtop.

▲ Although Dodge's fastback Charger looked little different in its second year, the '67 could now be had in R/T trim as shown here. Sales plummeted to just 15,788 for the year.

▲ Full-size '67 Fords followed the industry trend to cleaner lines with a handsome restyle. This $3493 Galaxie 500/XL ragtop, which came with the 289-inch V-8, is one of 5161 built.

▲ The first Hurst/Olds bowed in 1968 as a limited-production coupe, pillared or hardtop, based on the 4-4-2. The 515 that were built featured a special 390-horse 455 V-8, Turbo Hydra-Matic, Hurst Dual Gate shifter, heavy-duty everything, H/O emblems, and a special black-and-silver paint job.

▲ A new look was featured on midsize 1968 Pontiac two-doors, which moved to a tighter 112-inch wheelbase. This $2786 Le Mans hardtop coupe, of which 110,036 were built, wears optional Rally wheels and redline tires.

This is one of 50 special lightweight Mustangs built to showcase the new Cobra Jet 428 V-8. The cars dominated the S/S class at the '68 NHRA internationals.

1968

The 1968 Buick Riviera featured minimal changes, with headlamps built within its altered face and a heavier weight.

▲ Besides setting records with the AMX, land-speed-record driver Craig Breedlove ran this Javelin at the Bonneville Salt Flats in Utah in August 1968.

▼ The 1968 Buick Riviera, now weighing 4222 pounds, hid its headlamps within a restyled face. Changes were few—and mostly dictated by government clean-air mavens.

1969

The Camaro Z/28 and Boss 429 Mustang set performance records. Muscle cars hit their peak in power and style.

▲ Continuing their muscle car collaboration, Hurst/Olds again offered a Cutlass-based hardtop coupe—the only body style this year—which ran with the huge 455-inch V-8 and gold-and-white paint. Horses numbered 380; cars built, 906.

▲ Like Chevy's Camaro, Pontiac's Firebird got a lower-body restyle for '69, but demand slumped to 76,059 hardtop coupes and 11,649 ragtops.

▼ "Here come da Judge," a new $332 option package for Pontiac's '69 GTO with a 366-horse "Ram Air III" 400-inch V-8 and loud "The Judge" decals.

▼ Like the GTO, lesser midsize Pontiacs wore only modest styling changes for 1969. This Le Mans convertible is equipped with the division's novel hood-mounted tachometer, as well as extra-cost wire wheel covers.

Although it wore a revised grille for '69, Plymouth's famous "Beep! Beep!" Road Runner shifted gears by emphasizing luxury options, such as bucket seats, console, and power windows.

◀ Shuffled trim, equipment, and color options were the main changes for AMC's 1969 Javelin, but sales dropped sharply to 40,675, with the base model suffering most of the loss. Here, the jazzy $2633 SST (23,286 were built) in early year trim with the popular vinyl top.

▼ A heavy lower-body restyle marked Chevy's Camaro "ponycars" for 1969. The Z/28 hardtop saw sales of 19,014.

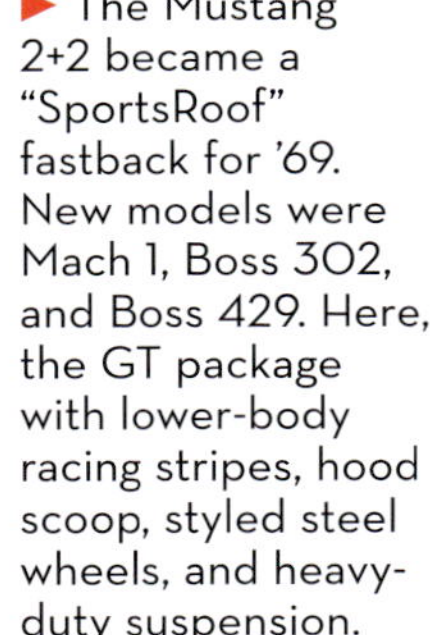

▶ The Mustang 2+2 became a "SportsRoof" fastback for '69. New models were Mach 1, Boss 302, and Boss 429. Here, the GT package with lower-body racing stripes, hood scoop, styled steel wheels, and heavy-duty suspension.

▶ Still pushing sporty big cars, Mercury revived the Marauder name for '69. This uplevel X-100 version was priced at $4091; 5635 were produced.

▲ Ford went chasing Plymouth's Road Runner for '69 with its new Torino Cobra, a budget muscle car with a 335-horse 428 Cobra Jet V-8. This seldom-seen notchback hardtop version started at a low $3164. Most Cobras were fastbacks.

1970

Plymouth's Superbird made a bold statement with its aerodynamic design and powerful engine. Built with precision and speed in mind, it quickly garnered attention.

Evolved from Dodge's 1969-only Charger Daytona, the 1970 Plymouth Superbird carried Chrysler's colors in NASCAR racing. Exactly 1920 were built, versus 505 Chargers. Together, they dominated the 1970 NASCAR racing season.

▼ Chevy unwrapped a handsome new Camaro coupe for mid 1970. This is one of three concept Z/28 "Sunshine Special" prototypes proposed by Hurst.

► Pontiac altered the GTO's styling for 1970, giving it a new Endura nose with exposed headlamps, bodyside creases, and a revised rump. Newly optional for regular GTOs, such as the ragtop pictured here, was a 360-bhp 455-cid V-8. That engine wasn't initially offered in the Judge (*left*), most of which used the 366-bhp 400-cid Ram Air III V-8. Total 1970 output came to 36,366 hardtops and 3783 ragtops.

▲ This "Panther Pink" Challenger T/A was one of 2539 built to qualify the new Dodge ponycar for Trans-Am racing. Street versions boasted a "Six Pak" (triple-carb) 340 small-block V-8, as the fender logo says. It developed 290 horses, double the 145 on base Slant Six models.

1971

Pontiac's full-size 1971 models perfected combined comfort and performance. The SS Chevelle continued as one of the best in the muscle car scene.

◀ AMC Javelins wore new styling for '71. The $3432 AMX, shown here, was now the high-performance Javelin. Top power choice was a new 401 V-8 with 330 horses; it cost $137 extra in the AMX.

▼ Though their faces were vaguely familiar, Pontiac's full-size '71s were all-new—and as big as American big cars would ever get. The pride of the line was a new top-line Grand Ville series that included this grandly priced $4706 convertible, which sold just 1789 units. A 325-horse 455-inch V-8 was the only engine offered.

▲▼ Buick made big changes for '71, starting with a bigger, all-new Riviera wearing controversial "boattail" fastback styling. At 33,810 units, sales of the $5253 hardtop coupe were down nearly 10 percent from 1970. Despite a three-inch-longer 122-inch wheelbase, the 4325-pound '71 Riv was little heavier than the 1966–70 models. The standard engine was a 315-horse V-8; a 330-bhp version was optional, as was a Gran Sport handling package.

◀ This base '71 GTO convertible is one of only 661 built; Judge ragtops, meanwhile, numbered a mere 17. Even base hardtop sales were little better at 9497 units.

◀ New low-compression engines gave '71 SS Chevelles slightly tamer performance, but cleaner exhaust pipes. Some 79,992 Super Sports were built, of which 19,292 had the big-block 454 option. An extra $485 bought 375 horses.

▼ The Ford Mustang grew to Clydesdale size in a full 1971 redesign. Topping Mach 1 as the top street performer was this new Boss 351, a fastback with a hot 330-horse 351 V-8.

▲ Formula remained a step down from Trans Am among performance Firebirds for 1971, but Pontiac added new 350 and 455 models to join the carryover Formula 400.

▼ A new nose marked Pontiac's 1971 GTOs, including "The Judge" hardtop coupe. This would be GTO's last year as a distinct series. Judge's 455-inch V-8 was down from 360 to 335 horses, while the base GTO's 400 V-8 dropped to 300.

▶ Plymouth purged midsize convertibles from its all-new '71 lineup. GTX remained the posh performer, a $3733 hardtop coupe. Only 2942 were sold, so it disappeared after '71.

AMC's sporty Javelin countered declining "go" with new "show," as on this AMX version specially ordered with the Pierre Cardin package. Overall Javelin sales eased about 1000 units to 26,184.

▲ Plymouth's Barracuda fell on hard times for '72, down to base and 'Cuda hardtops, with the latter's 340 small-block option the hottest available. Optional stripes and a "scooped" hood dressed up this base model, but real muscle cars didn't wear whitewalls.

◀ Chrysler added Newport Royal for 1971, and these continued little-changed for '72. All sold better than their costlier Newport Custom siblings. A 360-inch V-8 with 175 bhp was standard; Customs got a 400-inch mill with 190 horses.

▶ After two years, the Hurst/Olds returned for 1972 with a still-potent 455-inch V-8 at 300 net bhp. Just 629 were built.

1972

Horsepower ratings dropped as regulation tightened. The oil crisis loomed, threatening the future of performance cars.

▲ Once sporty, the Impala had been reduced to just a big, heavy boulevard cruiser by 1972. Base price dropped $42, to $3979, and production jumped from 4576 to 6456.

▲ Chevelle's SS package underwent few changes for 1972, but sales dropped to just under 25,000. A 307 V-8 was the base SS engine. Only 5333 cars got big-block 454s this year.

▲ Changes to Chevy's compact Nova were few. For '72, power choices were down to a standard 110-horse six, and optional 130-bhp 307-inch or 165-bhp 350-inch V-8s.

1973

The oil crisis hit, making big V-8s less practical. Compact and fuel-efficient cars gained popularity.

▲ Lincoln may have inspired the front redo on '73 Chryslers. Round headlamps in square bezels were a period design fad. The Royal was gone, so the base model was now simply Newport. This $4316 hardtop sedan found 20,175 customers.

▼ Pillared "Colonnade" rooflines marked an all-new fleet of 1973 GM intermediates. Among them were curvy Buicks, which got the revived Century name. This coupe has the $175 Gran Sport appearance and handling package.

▼ American Motors stylists under Dick Teague designed this sporty hatchback coupe to expand the Hornet compact line for 1973. Price: $2449.

▼ Midsize Plymouths met 1973 bumper rules with a new, more-restrained front end. Road Runner still hung in, but strictly as a thin-pillar coupe with V-8s of 318, 400, or 440 inches.

► Still around and still pretty potent in 1973 was Plymouth's 240-bhp Duster 340 fastback, pictured here with optional tape stripes and wider Rallye wheels.

Chevy's Corvette sported a revised profile for 1973, thanks to a restyled body-color front end that looked elegant and met the Feds' new five-mph bumper rule.

Against all odds, another Hurst/Olds bowed for '73, based on the new Cutlass Supreme coupe. Some 1097 were built, all with a 455 V-8 of about 250 net horsepower.

◄ This $4001 Polara Custom hardtop sedan, which found 29,341 buyers in 1973, came with a 150-horse 318-cubic-inch V-8, with options up to a 220-bhp 440-inch engine.

◄ Pontiac's '73 Firebirds showed no sign of crash bumpers, a tribute to GM designers. This $3276 Formula listed two 455-inch V-8s: a 250-horsepower HO and 310-horse Ram Air.

Looking to Bicentennial 1976, Chevy offered a "Spirit of America" trim option for several '74s, including the Vega.

▼ As if to answer its "What's a Matador" TV spots, AMC unwrapped this swollen coupe to replace pillarless hardtops for '74. This $3699 coupe is the sporty "X." Top engine: a 255-horse 401-inch V-8.

▲ An amalgam of styling cues, the AMC Javelin was also in its last year for '74. Sales: 29,536, 4980 of them hot AMXs.

▲ A revised tail with a five-mph bumper helped add 300 pounds to the 1974 Thunderbird, now 4825 pounds. A torquier 220-horse 460-inch V-8 replaced the standard 429.

▲ Well-timed to face the energy crisis, the all-new '74 Mustang II was 14.5-inches shorter and 300 pounds lighter than the old ponycar—and scored a resounding 385,993 sales. This posh $3480 Ghia came with an 88-bhp four, or optional 105-bhp V-6.

The 1974 Chevy Corvettes were the last with optional 454 big-block power—down to 270 bhp net—and the first with a restyled body-color rear end that neatly matched the previous year's new nose.

1974

The Mustang II launched with a smaller, less powerful design. Federal safety bumpers changed car styling.

1975

Catalytic converters became mandatory. Automakers struggled with emissions regulations.

▼ Cadillac's '75 Eldorado retained its basic '71 design, but got a wider grille with rectangular headlamps. As Caddy's only ragtop, this model found 8950 buyers.

▼ Satellites were renamed Furys for '75, but Plymouth's restyled midsize line still offered a Road Runner. It sold only 7183 copies despite available 440-inch V-8 power.

▶ The front-engine, rear-drive Bricklin SV-1 bowed in 1974 with gullwing doors and a price around $9800. Promoter Malcolm Bricklin billed it as a "Safety Vehicle," but most considered it a sports car. Early models used an AMC 360-cubic-inch V-8.

◀ The '75 would be the last Chevy Corvette convertible for 12 years. At $6537, just 4629 were built. With big-blocks killed off by emissions and economy concerns, Corvette power for '75 was handled by two 350-inch V-8s. Total sales rose to 38,465 units.

▲ Hornet hatchback coupes featured a big load opening and lots of carrying space. This 1975 has the sporty "X" option package. Top engine option was a 150-horse 304-inch V-8.

▲ Cast in the image of the great Shelby-Mustangs of the Sixties was a new $325 "Cobra II" option for 1976 Mustang II fastbacks. Included were nostalgic blue/white paint, louvered rear side windows, spoilers, snake insignia, and white-letter tires.

▼ One of Detroit's few genuine performance cars in 1976, Pontiac's Firebird Trans Am was up to $4987 without extras but enjoyed a sales surge to 46,701. This one wears the "screaming chicken" hood decal, a popular T/A option.

Mercury entered the expanding market for small sporty coupes by importing Ford of Europe's Capri in 1970. The line was renamed Ghia II in 1975. This is the posh Ghia model.

▲ Bowing for mid '75, the Oldsmobile Starfire was a clone of Chevy's Monza, but it ran with a Buick V-6 and offered no V-8. A $391 GT added stripes and improved handling.

◀ Bonneville resumed its flagship role by ousting Grand Ville as Pontiac's top 1976 full-size line. This is the base $5246 coupe, shown with vinyl roof and Rallye wheels.

1976

The Oldsmobile Starfire utilized both sporty performance and luxury features to appeal differing tastes. The Bonneville remained a staple in providing smooth, comfortable rides.

▲ Dodge's midsize line dropped the Coronet name for 1977 to become the "downsized" Monaco, while the former full-size Monaco was now "Royal Monaco." This top-line Brougham four-door sold for $4217, and 17,224 were sold.

▲ Dodge tried to recapture some of the aura of the muscle-car age with a new "Super Pak" option for '77 Aspens with the R/T package. Included were a rear spoiler, louvered side windows, heavy-duty suspension, and a performance axle

▲ For 1977, Ford Mustang II's Cobra II option offered new red/white and black/gold color schemes as well as blue/white. A $607 Sports Performance Package included a 139-bhp 302 V-8, four-speed, and heavy-duty chassis.

◀ Doing fair business for Buick since 1975 was the hatchback Skyhawk coupe, yet another version of Chevy's Monza, but with Buick's 231-cid V-6 power. The '77 wore a new crosshatch front in a quest for greater Buick identity.

▼ Billed as "The Next Generation of the Luxury Car," the 1977 C-body Cadillacs shared a new downsized platform with Buick and Olds. The $10,020 de Ville sedan (shown) and $9810 coupe enjoyed a sales surge to 234,171 units.

▲ Chevy's 1977 Corvette sported new black A-posts and front side lights. Price rose to $8648, but sales set a record for the second straight year: 49,213 units. Top mill was again a 210-bhp V-8.

1977

General Motors downsized its full-size cars. The industry adapted to new fuel economy standards.

▼ Midsize Chevys lost their 400-cid V-8 option for '77; a 170-bhp 350 was now the top choice. This was the last of the '73 "Colonnade" generation.

▲ Chevy's Monte Carlo was in the last year of its current design in 1977. Here, the top-line $5298 Landau. Lesser S models started at $4968.

▲ After a two-and-a-half-year furlough, Chevy recalled the Camaro Z28 as a mid-1977 package. A 350-cid V-8 and colorful graphics were included in the $5170 price. Sales were strong: 14,349.

▲ Esprit had been the "luxury" Firebird since 1970, and remained so for '77, when Pontiac's ponycars took on a handsome new "droop-snoot" nose. Both the $4551 Esprit (*shown*) and the $4270 base Firebird got a new standard engine, too: a 231-cid Buick V-6 rated at 105 bhp.

▲ AMC Gremlins for 1977 got an eggcrate grille and a four-cylinder base engine: an Audi-designed, 80-horse 2.0-liter built in Indiana. It was ordered in 20 percent of Gremlins.

AMC's not-so-subcompact Pacer broadened its appeal for '77 with three-door wagon models. This upper-level D/L wears optional woody-look trim. Wagon base price: $3799.

1978

Plymouth's Volaré provided a efficient ride with modern features. Dodge's Aspen was the epitome of performance.

▲ Thunderbird sales climbed 11 percent for '78, to 352,751. This $8420 Town Landau took a back seat to a $10,105 Diamond Jubilee model marking Ford Motor Company's 75th Anniversary.

◀ Corvette turned 25 in 1978 and celebrated by pacing that year's Indy 500. Chevy built 6502 pace car replicas like this, priced at $13,653.

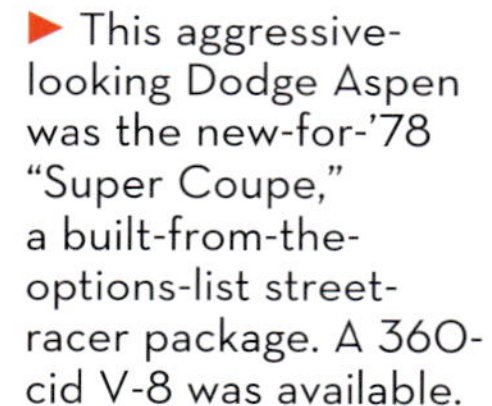

▶ This aggressive-looking Dodge Aspen was the new-for-'78 "Super Coupe," a built-from-the-options-list street-racer package. A 360-cid V-8 was available.

▲ Switching to GM's smaller new-generation A-body platform made Pontiac's 1978 Grand Prix the trimmest and lightest ever. Base, sporty SJ, and luxury LJ (*shown*) models all returned with better mileage, improved handling, and similar performance, despite smaller engines. Sales only held at their 1977 level—though that still meant a healthy 228,444 units.

◀ Like Dodge with Aspen, Plymouth issued a multitoned "Super Coupe" option on its '78 Volaré (*left*) for extroverted street racers. The Road Runner package was still around as a cousin to the Aspen R/T.

1979

The second oil crisis hit, increasing demand for smaller cars. American automakers faced growing competition from imports.

► Mustang came with four-cylinder, inline six, V-6, and V-8 engines. A Cobra model offered the best balance with its 140-horsepower, 2.3-liter turbocharged four.

▼ The 1979 Omni O24 was a new hatch coupe version of Dodge's L-body front-wheel-drive subcompact. Wheelbase was 2.5 inches shorter than the boxy five-door, which helped handling.

▼ Production of Ford's Pinto remained strong at 199,018 units in '79 despite headlines regarding exploding gas tanks. This hatch sedan wears the new-for-1978 $370 Rallye trim group.

◄ For 1979, Mercury opted for a version of Ford's redesigned Mustang to wear the Capri badge. It rejected Mustang's notchback coupe, but did offer base and luxury Ghia hatchbacks at $4872–$5237. A sporty RS package (*shown*) could be ordered with a turbo four, as on the Mustang Cobra.

◀ The Oldsmobile Toronado shed inches and pounds to become a more balanced personal-luxury coupe. The reward for Olds was sales that almost doubled from 1978 to just over 50,000.

▼ Pontiac's Firebird got yet another "facial" for '79. This is the racy Formula model, which had a base price of $6564 and could be ordered with a 220-bhp, 400-cid V-8.

▲ The '79 Mark V had a base price of $13,067. Designer packages like this Cartier ensemble added several hundred dollars to the sticker price. Sales perked up to 75,939 on word that 1979 would be the last year for a "big Mark."

◀ Despite few changes, the base price of Chevrolet's Corvette climbed to $12,313 for '79. Styling was little-altered from that of 1978's "glassback" makeover. Still, sales were the best ever for a single Corvette year: 53,807.

▶ The once-proud AMX name was hauled out for this 1979 "performance" version of AMC's new Spirit hatchback coupe. Priced at $6090, it attracted just 3657 buyers.

▼ General Motors's landmark X-body family of cars appeared in mid 1979 as 1980 models. The newly downsized compacts switched from rear drive to front-wheel drive. They also used transversely mounted inline four-cylinder and V-6 engines. Buick's 1980 Skylark offered two- and four-door notchbacks in base and luxury Limited trim. This Sport Coupe boasted black exterior trim and a sportive suspension. Skylark base prices ranged from $5342 to $6102 with the standard four-cylinder.

1980

Chrysler introduced front-wheel-drive economy cars. The industry shifted toward efficiency and downsizing.

◀ Chevy's 1980 Corvette shed 250 pounds via greater use of lightweight materials. The standard 350 V-8 was down to 170 net horses. Sales were down too, falling 13,200 units to 40,614.

◀ The Mercury Cougar line was pared to one $7045 XR-7 coupe for '80. It was a near-twin to the downsized Thunderbird. The wide rear-quarter roof shown here came in a new $1987 Luxury Group. Production was down to 58,028 units.

▲ For the look of performance but no extra power, the '80 Phoenix offered a sporty SJ option at $502 on notchbacks like this and $460 on hatchbacks. Pontiac's firmer Rally chassis was included. An early introduction helped push sales to 178,291 units.

◀ Chevy's small Monza sport coupes weren't changed much for 1980, and still had a standard 151 inline four and optional 231 V-6. This is the "2+2" fastback with the $531 Spyder package.

▶ A new 4.2-liter (255-cid) V-8 replaced the familiar 302 option in 1980 Ford Mustangs. This is the hatch coupe with a turbocharged four and optional Cobra package.

▲ Big 1980 Buicks emphasized economy with an "aero" nose and minor weight losses. Electras like this $10,537 Park Avenue coupe also boasted a thriftier new 4.1-liter V-6 as standard.

▲ The Avanti II was still around in 1981, offering Raymond Loewy styling from Studebaker days nearly twenty years before. It switched Chevrolet engines, though, from a 190-bhp 350 V-8 to a 155-bhp 305—a sign of the times.

◀ Reshaped body contours and a revised engine lineup (including shelving the 350-cid gas V-8) helped improve fuel economy on 1980 full-size Pontiacs. This Bonneville Brougham sedan cost $8160; 21,249 were built.

► AMC's Spirit also offered Pontiac's 2.5-liter four as standard for 1981, and spawned four-wheel-drive Eagle Kammback and hatchback variants. Here a $5589 Spirit D/L.

◀ The second-generation Chevy Camaro would bow out after 1981 and sales of 126,139. The top-gun Z28 (*shown*) grabbed 43,272 of them at $8263 apiece. The optional 350-cid V-8 was available only with automatic transmission.

► Pontiac's '81 Grand Prix slicked down a tad for better mileage, but go power had got up and gone. A 120-bhp 265 V-8 was top dog. Here, the $7803 LJ model.

1981

The 1981 Pontiac Grand Prix struck a refined balance of performance and comfort while the Avanti II stuck around.

1982

The Pontiac Firebird received
aerodynamic redesigns
Performance cars
slowly made a comeback.

◀ With aggressive looks and better handling in a trimmer package, the 1982 debut of the third-generation Pontiac Firebird Trans Am was a success. Sales rose to 52,960 units.

▼ Chevrolet had a new Celebrity for 1982: a trimmer front-wheel-drive midsize workhorse to supplement the rear-drive Malibu. This coupe and a sedan were offered at $8313 to $8588.

J2000 was the "alphanumeric" tag for Pontiac's version of the new 1982 GM J-car, offered in the same four body types as the Chevy Cavalier. The SE hatch coupe (shown) was base priced at $7654.

▲ Though little-changed for '82, the Mark VI was no longer badged Continental. The label was transferred to that year's new compact Lincoln sedan. But trim variations for the Mark continued without end. Witness this $23,594 Bill Blass coupe in new red/white livery with standard wire wheels.

▲ Bowing in spring 1982 to replace the Starfire, Firenza was Oldsmobile's version of GM's new J-car subcompact. It differed from Chevy's Cavalier in having a standard overhead-cam 1.8-liter four-cylinder engine.

▲ The biggest news for Plymouth's subcompact Horizon was a new top-line Custom, shown here with optional two-tone paint. The sporty TC3 two-door carried over unchanged.

Plymouth revived the Scamp name for its new 1983 twin to Dodge's Rampage pickup. But it didn't sell nearly as well, and was dropped after one year and production of only 2129 units.

▼ A standard five-speed manual gearbox, new four-speed automatic option, and more engine choices highlighted Pontiac's 1983 Firebirds. Here, the midline $10,322 S/E. Tougher competition cut F-Bird sales more than 50 percent to 74,884.

► The 1983 Thunderbird dramatically signaled Ford Motor Company's turn to clean, low-drag styling. The standard model offered V-6 or V-8 power for $9000–$10,000.

◄ After reviving a truly hot GT for 1982, Ford made Mustang even more sporty with an aero-look facelift, as displayed on this coupe, as well as reborn ragtops.

1983

Automakers embraced slimmer designs, upgrade in performance, and fuel efficiency. From Plymouth's Scamp to Ford's Thunderbird, there was a balanced between innovation and style.

◄ The rear roofline was the biggest visual difference between the '83 Mercury Cougar and Ford Thunderbird. The cat wore an upright backlight for the more formal look thought to be favored by Mercury buyers. This LS Cougar had a base price of $10,850; the standard model started at $9521.

▲ Like Ford's EXP, Mercury's two-seat LN7 gained a high-output engine for '83, but sales sank from 35,000 to just 4528.

1984

The Chevrolet Corvette C4 brought high-tech performance. Ford prepared to relaunched the Mustang with a new design.

Only 50 ASC/McLaren Capris were built for 1984, each with a $25,000 sticker. A 302-inch V-8 was standard.

▼ Appearing in late 1984 as '85 models were new Twentieth Anniversary Signature Series Excaliburs. The run consisted of 50 Phaetons (*shown*) and 50 Roadsters.

◀ First-year Mark VII sales were 33,344, up almost 3000 over the '83 Mark VI. Surprisingly popular was this new $23,706 LSC (Luxury Sport Coupe) with "more European" features.

◀ Despite being emissions-limited to a Chevrolet 155-horse 305-cid V-8, Series IV Excaliburs were undeniably unique, especially when ordered as the rumble-seat Roadster.

◀ The first new Chevrolet Corvette in 15 years debuted in early '83 as a 1984 model. Lighter and smaller than the old "shark," it arrived stickered at $21,800—up a cool $3510—with a 205-horsepower V-8. Sales zoomed to 51,547.

▲ Ford's 1985 Thunderbirds wore a slightly different grille, bigger "boots," and new instrumentation. Sales dipped to 151,851 units. This Turbo Coupe now stickered at $13,365.

▲ Ford boosted its 1985 Mustang SVO to 205 horses, but sales still stalled, dropping by half to 1954 units—despite a base price reduction to $14,251. Ponycar buyers wanted V-8s.

▲ Like its near-identical cousin Ford LTD Crown Victoria, the big Mercury Grand Marquis was still quite popular in 1985, racking up some 161,258 sales. Here, the upper-level $12,789 LS coupe. Standard coupes started at $12,240.

▲ A new dash and minor trim changes carried Mercury's Cougar through 1985, with demand down slightly to 117,274 units. This top-line turbocharged XR-7 sold for $13,599.

▲ Despite many enhancements, Mercury's 1985 Capri languished, racking up just 18,657 total sales. This sporty RS hatchback included the 5.0L V-8 in its $10,223 base price.

◀ The rear-drive '85 Olds Delta 88 offered more metal for the money than the new front-drive Ninety Eight. Sales neared 242,000 units. Here, an $11,062 Royale Brougham LS.

1985

The Oldsmobile Delta 88 gave a smooth ride with a spacious interior. Mercury's Grand Marquis became a top contender in the sedan market.

▲ Still fighting a horde of Japanese small cars, the AMC-built 1985 Renault Alliance sported a new face and taillamps, plus a 50-month/50,000-mile powertrain warranty. Sales of L and DL ragtops totaled just 2015 units.

▼ Pontiac's Grand Am would prove to be the most consistently popular GM front-drive N-body compact. Like the others, it bowed for '85 in base and uplevel coupe models only.

▲ After topping Detroit's 1984 sales chart, Chevy's Cavalier offered a zesty new Z24 option for 1985. It ran with a 125-horse V-6, as on this coupe.

◀ The hatchback Renault Encore shared the 1985 Alliance's new 77-horse 1.7 engine option. This top-line LS five-door sold from $7310, a bit less than the Alliance Limited.

When Camaro became the official car of the International Race of Champions, Chevy offered the IROC-Z for 1985. Base price: $11,739.

▲ The hot-selling Dodge Caravan moved into 1985 with newly available "convert-a-bed" rear seats and an overhead console. Here, the midline SE.

1986

The Ford Taurus revolutionized sedan design. Digital dashboards and fuel economy were major selling points.

▶ The return of Chevy's Corvette convertible symbolized a new renaissance in Detroit style and performance. This 'Vette paced the 1986 Indianapolis 500. Base price was $32,032.

Chrysler's 1986 LeBarons got a new engine option: a 2.5-liter version of the 2.2 "Trans-4." This Town & Country ragtop in Mark Cross trim was one of just 501 built for the year.

▲ Buick's Riviera was again downsized for 1986, and plunged 70 percent in sales. This sporty T-Type edition listed for a healthy $21,577.

▶ New for 1986 was this De Ville Touring Sedan (and Coupe). They came with a handling suspension and slightly less gingerbread.

▲ Widely previewed throughout 1985, the smooth, all-new '86 Ford Taurus not only replaced the dated Fairmont-based "little" LTD, but proved a much better seller. With front drive, three trim levels, sedan and wagon body styles, and a host of sensible features, Taurus became a symbol of Detroit's new "can-do" attitude. Base prices were in the $10,000–$14,000 range.

 100 YEARS OF AMERICAN CARS

◀ After adding four-doors like its '86 N-body sisters, Pontiac's Grand Am went sportier for '87 with a new 165-horse turbo 2.0-liter four option and an improved dash.

◀ Notchback '87 Pontiac Fieros like this SE got the nose of the mid-'86 fastback-profile GT, and all models came with a standard five-speed instead of four-speed manual.

▼ Roller valve lifters added 10 horses to give the '87 Chevrolet Corvette 240 in all. Some 10,625 ragtops and 20,007 coupes found buyers this year.

◀ The best-selling of GM's A-body quartet, Cierra enjoyed a new one-piece composite headlamps for 1987. A 3.8-liter V-6 was again the top power option, offering 150 horsepower.

▼ The 1987 Pontiac Firebird dropped its SE model, but still hewed to tradition with four models. Here they are (*clockwise from top left*): base coupe, Formula, Trans Am, and GTA. Newly standard for GTA and optional on Formula and T/A was the 5.7-liter V-8, rated at 210 horsepower.

1987

Buick's Grand National GNX made a lasting impressions with its turbocharged V-6 engine.

▲ The front-drive Dodge Daytona got its first major restyle for 1987, and expanded to base, new luxury Pacifica, and Shelby Z (*shown*) models. For all that, sales fell to 33,104.

▼ Built just for California in 1987 was a Camaro RS, a Z28 pretender packing (for insurance purposes) a mild V-6. The price was milder too, just $12,411.

Like its Dodge Caravan twin, the 1987 Plymouth Voyager added stretched "Grand" models. The Grand soon vied for sales honors with standard Voyagers, like this midline SE.

▲ Following an '83 facelift, Ford's Mustang was again restyled for 1987. GTs, like this $15,724 ragtop, were more "aero" than base models, thanks to new rocker skirts and "mini-blind" taillamps. Sales dropped roughly 40 percent to 159,145.

▼ Plymouth shadowed Dodge's new compacts with Sundance models that differed mainly in grille and taillamp designs. Even prices were in the same $7800–$7900 range.

An extra 10 horses couldn't keep Buick's 1987 Riviera, here a $22,181 T-Type, from record-low sales of just 15,223 units.

▶ A new marketing tack spelled the end of Buick's "modern muscle" GNX after 1987, when 547 were built. But these were the hottest of all, with 276 horses and blinding 4.7-second 0–60-mph ability. Base price was near $30,000.

1988

The Buick Regal was design and performance united. The LX appearance package of Plymouth's Voyager caught eyes.

◀ The new Cutlass Supreme arrived as one of 1988's front-drive GM10 coupes. Olds listed base, SL, and this sporty International Series variant. Sales reached nearly 95,000.

▼ Showing its best shape in years, the Pontiac Grand Prix was all-new for 1988. As one of the front-drive GM10 models, it boasted all-independent suspension and no less room than the old rear-drive GP. GM had finally learned the folly of "cookie-cutter" styling, and it paid off: Grand Prix sales rose five-fold to 86,357. Here, a sporty top-line SE. A 2.8-liter V-6 was standard.

▲ There was no reason for much change in the hot-selling Voyager minivan for 1988, but Plymouth offered a new LX appearance package. Here, a base-trim standard model.

▲ One of three all-new front-drive GM10 coupes, the 1988 Buick Regal featured Custom and Limited models, but options allowed building a "Gran Sport" version like this.

▲ This '88 turbocharged Lancer Shelby was new to Dodge's H-body line—and rare, with only 279 built. Based on the '86 Lancer Pacifica, it came only in monochrome white or red.

▲ After spending $100 million to develop a new suspension for 1988, GM killed the Pontiac Fiero. This Formula was one of the final 26,402 Fieros built.

▶ Pontiac's 1988 Firebird engine roster was Sixties-confusing, but the venerable Trans Am (*shown*) still had fire with a choice of three V-8s and from 170 to 225 horses. Styling across the board was little-changed from a mild 1987 facelift.

▲ The first front-drive Pontiac Bonneville returned from '87 in LE and SE trim, plus this aggressive new 1988 SSE. The SSE boasted a "3800" V-6 and antilock brakes for $21,879.

▼ Marking Trans Am's twentieth year were 1500 copies of this $25,000 '89 model with a 245-horse turbo V-6 from Buick's late GNX. It did 0–60 mph in just 5.4 seconds. It served as that year's Indy pace car with no engine modifications. Former Indy winner Bobby Unser is pictured here.

▲ Olds dropped a new high-output Quad-4 engine with 185 horses into Cutlass Calais coupes and sedans to create the even-sportier 1989 International Series models.

► Pontiac built 1000 special Grand Prixs in 1988 as McLaren Turbos. They inspired the regular-production Grand Prix Turbo for '89, with a similar intercooled 205-horse V-6 and racy body addenda. Prices started at around $26,000.

◄ The Oldsmobile Toronado hit a new sales low for 1989 with just 9877 orders. Only 3734 were standard $21,995 Toros like this; the $24,995 Trofeo accounted for the balance.

1989

Pontiac and Oldsmobile pushed peformance with turbocharged specials and high-output engineering.

▲ Still one of America's top sellers, the Ford Taurus returned for 1989 with a hot new 220-horse SHO sedan. Workaday models like this LX wagon no longer offered four-cylinder power, but the standard 3.0 and optional 3.8 V-6s continued.

▲ Ford's Mustang turned 25 in 1989, but persistent rumors of a hot rod anniversary model proved false. Sales held steady at a still-healthy 209,769, including 42,244 ragtops. Here, the $13,272 V-8-powered GT hatchback coupe.

▼ Rolled out as an early 1990 model, Chevy's new Corvette ZR-1 (*foreground*) boasted a wider tail with square lights, ultrawide tires, and an amazing new 375-horse 5.7-liter V-8. Its new six-speed manual gearbox was shared with the "basic" 'Vette. Corvette ZR-1's "LT-5" V-8 featured an all-aluminum design with port fuel injection and twin overhead cams on each cylinder bank working a total of 32 valves. A special dual induction system with electronic control featured a "valet" key that locked out ultimate power for unauthorized—or less-experienced—users.

▲ Cadillac's 1989 Allanté received a new 200-horse 4.5-liter V-8, variable-rate shock absorbers, and standard antitheft alarm. Sales rose modestly from the previous year's 2569 to 3296.

New "faces" freshened up the 1989 Dodge Daytonas, including this top-of-line Shelby model (no longer a "Z") with a 174-horse 2.2-liter "Turbo II" four engine.

▲ Mercury used the T-Bird's basic all-new design for 1989. Base LS and sporty XR-7 were offered. XR-7 returned to assisted aspiration, sharing T-Bird SC's supercharged V-6.

1990

Pontiac's Grand Am provided a sportier look coupled with an enhanced engine. Buick's Reatta delivered a unique ragtop design.

◀ Pontiac's 1990 Grand Am boasted one big update: a new high-output Quad-4 engine with 180 horses standard in SE models like this one. Grand Am saw 197,020 cars built.

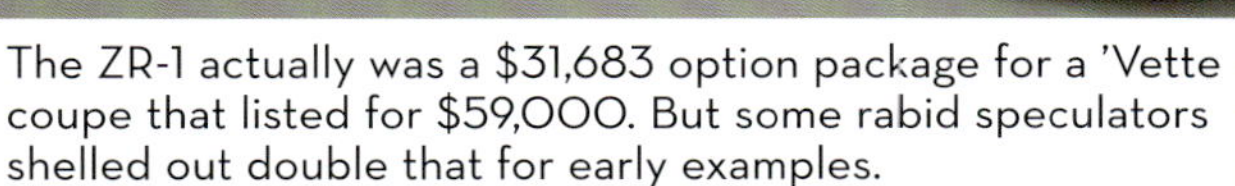

The ZR-1 actually was a $31,683 option package for a 'Vette coupe that listed for $59,000. But some rabid speculators shelled out double that for early examples.

▲ Pontiac Firebirds got a driver-side airbag for '90. Trans Am GTA remained the hottest—and was even hotter because its 5.7-liter V-8 gained 10 horses, to 235.

◀ Buick unveiled a ragtop Reatta for 1990 after a year's delay. But stickered at $35,000, it proved even tougher to sell than the coupe, and only 2437 would be built through 1991.

▼ In January 1991, after the release of a Chevy Camaro ragtop, Pontiac unwrapped its first Firebird convertibles since '69, complete with a new nose inspired by the 1988 Pontiac Banshee show car. The reborn ragtop came in base or Trans Am trim, starting at $19,159. Only about 2000 were built for that model year.

▲ Plymouth's 1991 Acclaim lost its turbo option but gained available antilock brakes. This top-line LX again came with 3.0 V-6 engine and four-speed "Ultradrive" automatic.

▲ Mercury Cougar XR7 reverted to a conventional V-8 for 1991: a 200-bhp version of the venerable 302 borrowed from Mustang GT and Lincoln Mark VII. Base price was up to $20,905, versus $15,629 for the entry 3.8 V-6 LS model.

1991

The Buick Regal showcased a contemporary look. The practical Plymouth Acclaim was designed to meet demand.

▲ After eight long years and $8 billion in start-up costs, GM's much-anticipated new Saturn subcompacts debuted for 1991 with four four-cylinder models: twincam SC coupe and SL2 sedan (*foreground*), and single-cam SL and SL1 sedans (*SL1 background*). Interest was high with prices as low as $7995, but a deliberate "go-slow" policy held total production to 48,629 for the model year.

A new tapered nose graced the 1991 Chevy Corvettes, and standard models got the same rear-end look as the pricey ZR-1—to the dismay of early Z buyers.

▲ Buick's Regal entered 1991 with cosmetic tweaks and a 170-horse 3.8 V-6 as an upgrade to the standard 140-bhp 3.1. Base price on this Limited coupe was up to $16,455.

▼ The $20,999 supercharged SC remained Ford's top T-Bird for '91, but the big news was optional 302 V-8 power for base and midrange LX models, with 200 horses.

◀ A larger 3.8-liter version of Chrysler's 3.3 V-6 was newly standard for the '91 Imperial. It gave only three more horses (150 total), but was torquier. Sales slipped to just 11,601.

1992

The 1992 Crown Victoria became a staple in American full-size sedans, while Lincoln's Mark VII continually improved.

◀ Cadillac's two-door Eldorado wore its own new design for 1992, growing 11 inches longer on an unchanged wheelbase. Its 200-horse 4.9-liter V-8 was carried over intact. Just over 31,000 Eldos found buyers in '92. Base price: $32,470.

◀ Chevy passed a major milestone in 1992 by building its one-millionth Corvette, a white convertible with that year's new 5.7 LT1 V-8, which replaced the old like-size L98 as base powerplant. Also new that year: standard six-speed manual gearbox, optional ASR ("Acceleration Slip Regulation") traction control, and extra-cost "Quiet Car Package." Here, the historic millionth 'Vette poses with a 1953 original at the Bowling Green, Kentucky, Corvette plant, which hosted 'Vette owners and their cars in a week-long celebration.

▼ The 1992 Crown Victoria debuted in March '91 with smooth looks, reworked rear-drive chassis, and Ford's new 4.6 "modular" V-8 with 190 bhp. This police package countered Chevy Caprice's similar 9C1 group.

▲ With an all-new replacement just around the corner, 1992 was the end for Lincoln's Mark VII, which was down to just a Bill Blass edition and the ever-sporty LSC (*shown*). Both listed at around $32,000. Total model-year production was a mere 5732.

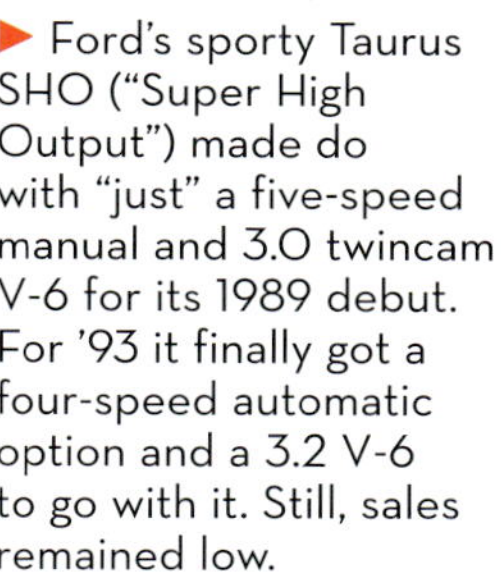

▶ Ford's sporty Taurus SHO ("Super High Output") made do with "just" a five-speed manual and 3.0 twincam V-6 for its 1989 debut. For '93 it finally got a four-speed automatic option and a 3.2 V-6 to go with it. Still, sales remained low.

▲ Though still a cousin of Mazda's MX-6, the 1993 Ford Probe was all-new, again with unique styling and its own chassis tuning. Both the base four-cylinder hatch coupe and this sporty V-6 GT proved popular, scoring 137,422 sales.

▶ With more than 247,000 sales, the Pontiac Grand Am bowed only to the Chevrolet Cavalier as General Motors's most-popular 1993 car. That year's models were much like the fully revised '92s, but received new engine mounts and induction systems for quieter four-cylinder operation, plus a firmer "Level III" sports suspension for the top-line GT sedan and coupe (*shown*).

◀ Having gained mini-headlamps in a 1992 facelift, the Cutlass Supreme convertible offered a "Twin Dual Cam" 3.4-liter V-6 as a new option in Oldsmobile's 95th anniversary year. Base price for the drop top: $22,699.

1993

Ford's '93 Probe delivered a youthful, sporty look. The Taurus SHO's V-6 engine pushed the abilities of sedans.

◀ A 1988 newcomer based on the Mazda 323, the subcompact Mercury Tracer was redesigned for '91 along with Ford's second-series Escort. The '93 lineup again included a sporty LTS four-door, with a twincam 1.8-liter Mazda four. Base price: $12,023.

▲ Mercury joined the minivan melee with the 1993 Villager, sharing a front-drive design with the new Ford-built Nissan Quest. A V-6 and four-speed automatic were standard on GS and this uplevel LS at prices from $17,000. Sales were good at close to 109,000.

◀ Mercury's big Grand Marquis sedan was fully revamped along with Ford's Crown Victoria for 1992, losing wagons but gaining a modern new drivetrain. For 1993, the LS (*shown*) and entry-level GS got a standard passenger air-bag and minor equipment changes.

▲ Formula was the bargain performance buy among 1993 Pontiac Firebirds, offering the Trans Am's 275-horse LT1 V-8 and six-speed manual gearbox for about $3400 less to start: $17,995. All the new 'Birds boasted antilock brakes and styling inspired by the '88 Banshee show car.

◀ A fourth-generation Firebird bowed for 1993 with the same basic design as the new Camaro, but Pontiac offered two V-8 models—Formula and Trans Am—to Chevy's one, plus a V-6 base car. Here, the Trans Am.

▶ The new '94 Mustang was built on a heavily modified version of the old '79-vintage "Fox" chassis, but boasted all-new styling inside and out, plus standard all-disc brakes with optional anti-lock control. Here, the bespoilered $20,160 GT coupe.

◀ As promised, ragtop Chevy Camaros returned for 1994 in new fourth-generation guise. Like the coupes, the convertibles came in V-6 base form and high-performance V-8 Z28 (*shown*). A power top with glass rear window was included on both. Camaro was otherwise little-changed, but traction control was a new mid-season option for Z28s with automatic.

▶ Chevy's Corvette added traction control and a passenger airbag as new standard equipment for 1994. The hot ZR-1 returned from '93 with 405 horses versus its previous 375, but remained a tough sell. Here, the dashing $42,960 ragtop.

GM's Saturn brand had expanded the family by '94 to include "SW" wagons (*front*) and a lower-priced SC1 coupe.

▲ The Japanese-built Dodge Stealth continued into 1994 as close kin to Mitsubishi's 3000GT. Tops among the three available models was this racy $37,500 R/T Turbo with a turbocharged 3.0-liter V-6 sending 320 horses to all four wheels.

1994

The Dodge Stealth's aggressive styling made it stand out in the sports coupe market.

Supplanting Sunbird was Pontiac's Sunfire. Coupe models were this 120-bhp, $11,074 SE or the 150-bhp, $12,834 GT.

▼ Corvette paced the Indianapolis 500 for the third time in 1995, and celebrated with 527 near-replicas of the genuine pace car shown. With its 300-bhp LT1 V-8, the 'Vette needed no mechanical modifications to pace the big race.

▲ The redesigned Cavalier featured two- and four-door models, plus a convertible with power top. Priced at $17,210, it was the costliest Cavalier.

▼ Aurora bowed for '95 to signal a new direction for Oldsmobile. It targeted luxury imports and started at $31,370.

▼ The V-10, 400-bhp Viper continued mechanically unchanged for '95, though its cabin gained a passenger assist handle and seat-cushion storage pockets. Dodge had also begun to offer alternatives to the original red exterior/gray interior colors. Emerald Green and Bright Yellow were now offered, with a black-and-tan upholstery combination also available.

1995

Chevrolet redesigned its Cavalier so it had a more modern look with enhanced performance.

1996

Chrysler launched the Sebring, a stylish addition to the sedan market. Cadillac updated the De Ville with better technology.

◀ Dodge's Viper RT/10 roadster was joined in 1996 by the GTS coupe. Both used a V-10, but the new coupe had 450 bhp to the RT/10's 415. No modification was required for the GTS to pace that year's Indy 500. Dodge also supplied support trucks.

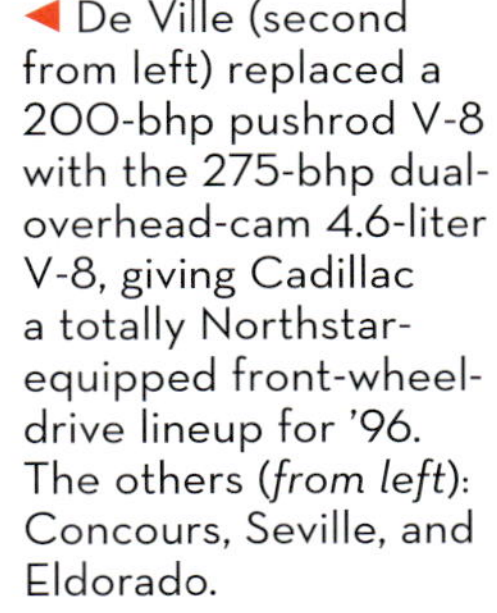

◀ De Ville (second from left) replaced a 200-bhp pushrod V-8 with the 275-bhp dual-overhead-cam 4.6-liter V-8, giving Cadillac a totally Northstar-equipped front-wheel-drive lineup for '96. The others (*from left*): Concours, Seville, and Eldorado.

Corvette's fourth generation went out with a flourish in '96, with silver Collector Editions and this very special Grand Sport. Just 1000 of the latter were built and they used a 330-bhp LT4 V-8. Other 'Vettes had the slightly less-potent 300-bhp LT1.

▶ Borrowing Corvette's 5.7-liter LT1 V-8, albeit detuned to 285 bhp for '96, was the Chevy Camaro Z28. It was hot enough to pace NASCAR's third Brickyard 400. Base Camaros, meanwhile, traded their 160-bhp 3.4-liter V-6s for smoother 200-bhp 3.8-liter units.

▲ Revised front and rear styling and 240 bhp for the supercharged V-6 (up by 15) were Bonneville's 1996 changes.

▼ Replacing the LeBaron as Chrysler's ragtop was the '96 Sebring. Sebring coupes used a Mitsubishi platform, but the attractive new convertible was built off Chrysler's own JA chassis.

1997

The Chevrolet Corvette C5 launched with a new LS1 V-8. Gas prices remained low, keeping big vehicles popular.

▶ Base Parks used the 205-bhp 3.8-liter V-6 and started at $29,995. The Ultra (*shown*) included the 240-bhp supercharged 3.8, plus traction control and goodies in its $34,995 base price. Sales jumped 30 percent, to 68,777.

◀ Chevrolet redesigned its two-seat sports car for '97, retaining a rear-wheel-drive layout, fiberglass body panels, and V-8 power, but changing most everything else. A hatchback coupe with a removable roof panel debuted first. Wheelbase grew by 8.3 inches, to 104.5, but body length increased just 1.2 inches. A new chassis eliminated the tall frame rails of the previous generation, making it easier to get into and out of the spaciously redesigned cabin. Underhood was a new all-aluminum 5.7-liter pushrod V-8 with 345 bhp. The transmission—six-speed manual or four-speed automatic—was relocated to the rear axle, for better weight distribution and more interior room. At $37,495 to start, the fifth-generation 'Vette had Ferrari-like performance: 0–60 mph in 4.7 seconds and a 172-mph top speed.

◀ For '97, Park Avenue moved to the rigid new platform GM introduced on the Buick Riviera and Olds Aurora. Styling retained traditional Park Avenue themes, but the wheelbase grew by three inches, weight by 250 pounds.

▶ Redesigned for '97, Buick's Century retained its conservative appeal but wrapped it in new sheet metal. Base models started at $17,845, Limiteds (*shown*) at $19,220. Both had a V-6.

◀ Sold by Chrysler Corporation's Jeep-Eagle division, the Mitsubishi-made Talon accounted for 10,206 of Eagle's 15,352 sales in 1997. The Vision sedan made up the balance. This is the front-drive, 140-bhp, $14,830 Talon ESi.

▶ The huge rear-drive Fleetwood was dead, leaving the $36,995 De Ville to carry Cadillac's big sedan torch. De Ville got standard side airbags and a subtle facelift for 1997.

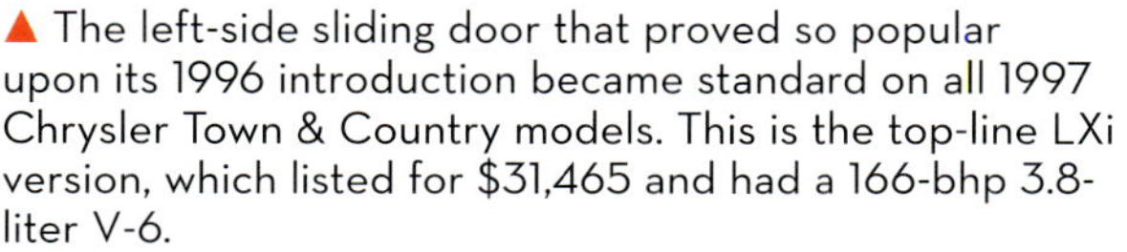

▲ The left-side sliding door that proved so popular upon its 1996 introduction became standard on all 1997 Chrysler Town & Country models. This is the top-line LXi version, which listed for $31,465 and had a 166-bhp 3.8-liter V-6.

▲ Dodge's Stratus had racing in its blood. Its competition iteration finished first and second in the 2.0-liter class in the short-lived North American touring car series. Like production versions, the racers were front-wheel drive.

▲ Caravan sales slipped five percent coming off its '96 redesign, but Dodge still had America's best-selling minivan in 1997, with 285,736 units. This is the Grand Caravan LE: $25,825 with front-wheel drive, $28,870 with AWD.

▲ Chrysler Corporation design chief Tom Gale was a fan of true hot rods, and company vice chairman Robert Lutz was a "car guy." They put their money where their hearts were by championing the transformation of the Prowler from a show car to a 1997 production Plymouth. Sticker price was $38,300, but demand for the limited-edition, rear-wheel-drive two-seater pushed some early buyers to pay double that.

Owners loved them, but aged Saturns attracted fewer buyers for '97. Sales fell 10 percent, to 251,099.

▶ Both the Viper GTS coupe and RT/10 roadster now had the same 450-bhp version of the 8.0-liter (488-cid) V-10.

▲ Grand Am was in the last year of its 1992–1998 incarnation, and though sales fell 13 percent for '98, it remained Pontiac's best-selling model. This is the GT coupe. Price: $16,324

The WS6 Ram Air option added $3100 to the $22,865 Firebird Formula (*shown*), the $25,975 Trans Am coupe, or $29,715 convertible. It boosted the 5.7-liter V-8 from 305 bhp to 320.

▲ Chevrolet's big sport-utility Tahoe wasn't a hit with police, but Camaro's pursuit package, which could be had with the Z28's sport suspension and 305-bhp Corvette-derived 5.7-liter V-8, was just the ticket for highway patrol duty.

1998

The Pontiac Firebird WS6 Ram Air delivered more power, and the Chevrolet Camaro patrolled the highways of the United States.

▲ America's best-selling convertible was again the Chrysler Sebring, though about half its 40,000 annual sales were to rental fleets.

◀ Corvette's new convertible needed no mechanical modifications to pace the '98 Indy 500. It posed with the three other 'Vettes to do the honors.

1999

The Mustang reached 35 years—marking a milestone and demonstrating lasting popularity.

◀ Chevy's Corvette added a lightweight hardtop body style to its convertible and hatchback choices for 1999. The hardtop (*foreground*) shared the other models' 345-bhp V-8, but not luxury options new to them: a head-up instrument display and a power telescoping steering column.

◀ New-for-'99 was this luxury version of the Chrysler Concorde. Called the LHS, its front and rear look was distinct from the Concorde, and it used a 253-bhp 3.5-liter version of Concorde's 225-bhp 3.2-liter V-6. Base price: $28,850.

▲ Ford's ponycar celebrated its 35th anniversary in 1999 with new styling and more power. The base model's 3.8-liter V-6 gained 40 bhp, to 190, and the GT's overhead-cam 4.6-liter V-8 gained 35 bhp, to 260. Traction control was a first-time option on these rear-drive coupes and convertibles. A wider rear track improved handling and four-wheel discs were newly standard. This is the $24,870 GT convertible.

◀ Town Car was America's only homegrown rear-wheel-drive luxury car and the Lincoln gained standard front side airbags for '99. Base prices ranged from $38,325 to $42,825.

Buick killed the Riviera early in the '99 model year. About 200 of the last 2000 built for the year were tagged Silver Arrows, after the original 1963 Riviera concept car. Riviera prices started at $33,820.

Cougar arrived for 1999 as a "new-edge" styled Mercury coupe built on the Contour/ Mystique platform.

▲ Plymouth's hot rod Prowler sat out '98, then returned for 1999 with a new 3.5-liter V-6 of 253 bhp, 35 more than the engine it replaced. Prowler now did 0–60 mph in six seconds, not seven. Black, yellow, or red paint added $1000. Hot rod touches included a steering-column-mounted tachometer and central gauges in a body-colored cove.

▲ Anticipating a redesign for 2000, the Pontiac Bonneville essentially stood pat for '99. This is the base SE model, which started at $22,800 and had a 205-bhp V-8 and standard ABS.

◀ Sedan and coupe Grand Ams returned with a standard 150-bhp twincam four-cylinder engine. Uplevel models, including this $18,970 SE coupe, got a 170-bhp 3.4-liter V-6.

▼ New for Chevy's Venture minivan was the Warner Bros. Edition. A standard second-row videotape player was part of the deal.

Jay Leno paced the 1999 Indy 500 in a 2000 Monte Carlo.

◀ Big changes for GMC's big rigs brought revised sheet metal and new engines for the 2000 model year. Twins to Chevrolet's Tahoe and Suburban, Yukon (*left*) and Yukon XL (*right*) enjoyed new "Gen III" V-8s that displaced 4.8, 5.3, and 6.0 liters.

2000

GMC updated the Yukon for those wanting a reliable and large SUV. Automakers focused on technology and efficiency.

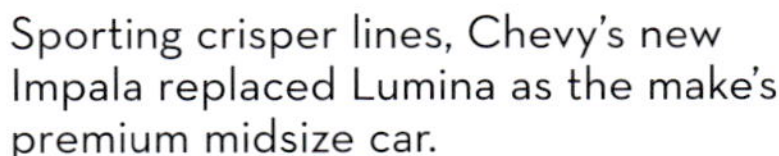

Sporting crisper lines, Chevy's new Impala replaced Lumina as the make's premium midsize car.

▲ When shown at Detroit's 2000 North American International Auto Show in January, Ford's retro-styled Thunderbird concept looked production ready.

▲ ► Clinging to its extroverted nature, the redesigned Bonneville retained most of its brash styling cues for 2000. The SSEi (*below right*) sported a 240-horsepower 3.8-liter V-6.

2001

Fuel efficiency regulations tightened further, which made interest in vans like the Dodge Caravan increase.

▲ ▶ Although the rear-drive Ford Crown Victoria still dominated the police market, a growing number of law-enforcement fleets were adding Chevy's front-drive Impala (*above*) to their rolling stock. Monte Carlo (*right*) earned pace car honors at the 2000 Brickyard 400. Just 1300 replicas were built.

◀ A fresh face and more muscle arrived for Dodge Caravan in 2001. The top engine option was a 215-horsepower 3.8-liter V-6, up 35 for the new year.

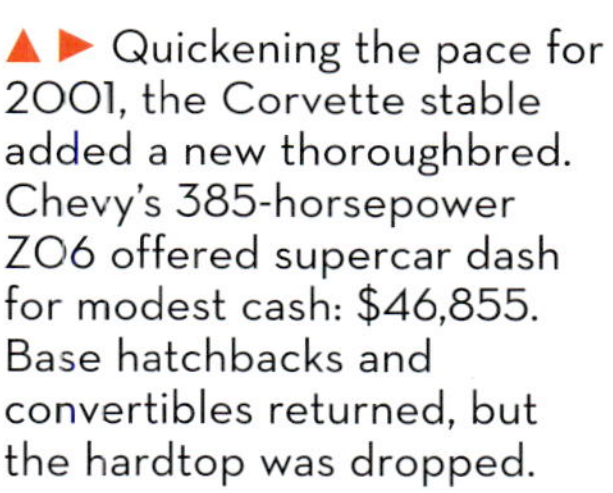

▲ ▶ Quickening the pace for 2001, the Corvette stable added a new thoroughbred. Chevy's 385-horsepower Z06 offered supercar dash for modest cash: $46,855. Base hatchbacks and convertibles returned, but the hardtop was dropped.

▲ Redesigned for 2002, Dodge's full-size Ram pickups lost none of their "big rig" presence. Extended cabs disappeared, leaving only regular- and Quad-cab body styles.

▲▼ Though Ford still had a lock on the police-car market, Dodge made a credible pitch to fleet buyers with its shapely Intrepid (*above*). With the Plymouth brand now a historical footnote, the hot rod Prowler (*below*) was moved to Chrysler.

◄▼ An SS 35th Anniversary Edition marked Camaro's last year in the Chevy lineup. Slow sales may have hastened the demise of the storied ponycar, but performance remained brisk. The Corvette-derived V-8 delivered 325 horsepower in SS models.

▲ GM supplemented its line of midsize SUVs with three new trucks in 2003. GMC Envoy (*left*), Oldsmobile Bravada (*middle*), and Chevy TrailBlazer (*right*) boasted spacious interiors and a 270-horsepower inline six.

2002

The Chevrolet Camaro and Pontiac Firebird were discontinued. SUVs continued dominating sales.

2003

The Corvette remained as a high-performance supercar. Hybrid cars gained traction.

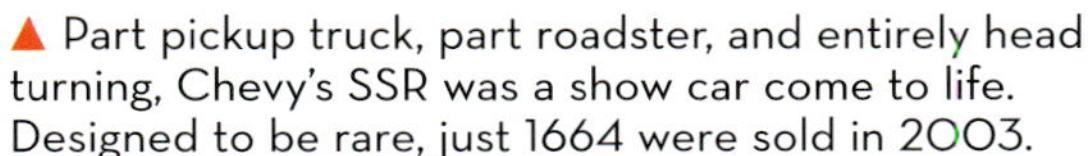

▲ Part pickup truck, part roadster, and entirely head turning, Chevy's SSR was a show car come to life. Designed to be rare, just 1664 were sold in 2003.

◀ ▲ A retractable hardtop and two-place seating characterized the brash SSR, as did its $42,000 price. Based on GM's midsize SUV chassis, SSR was too heavy to be truly sporty. A 300-horsepower V-8 provided the thrust.

◀ ▶ The new Escalade ESV (*left*) added 12 inches to Cadillac's popular SUV. Bulgari-designed instrumentation (*right*) added elegance and helped distinguish Escalade from GM's other big trucks.

◀ Chevy's legendary two-seater turned 50 in 2003. All '03 Corvettes got commemorative badging to mark the occasion, but the $5000 50th Anniversary Package upped the ante with unique trim, special wheels, and magnetic ride control. The Z06 was still king of the hill, but standard 'Vettes were no slouches, boasting 350 horses.

◀ Lincoln's big Navigator got a baby brother in 2003, the Ford Explorer-based Aviator. Prices started at $39,225.

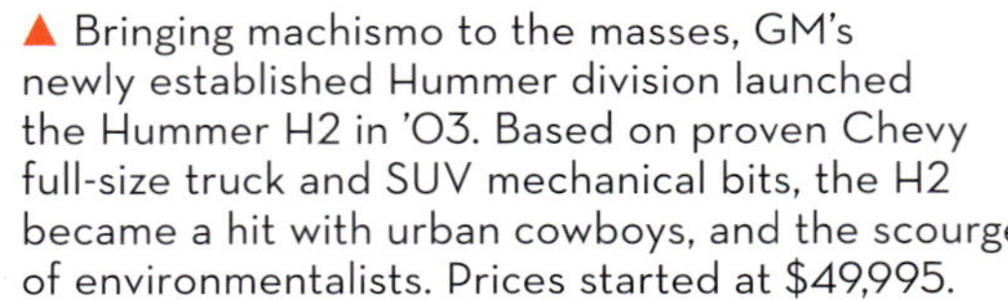

▲ Bringing machismo to the masses, GM's newly established Hummer division launched the Hummer H2 in '03. Based on proven Chevy full-size truck and SUV mechanical bits, the H2 became a hit with urban cowboys, and the scourge of environmentalists. Prices started at $49,995.

▲ Still plastic clad, Saturn's smallest car was all new for 2003 and renamed: Ion. Rear-hinged back doors afforded easy access to coupe interiors, while a flat-folding front passenger seat created extra space. Coupe prices started at $14,030.

▲ A blast from the past, the Mach 1 moniker was reborn after a 23-year hiatus. Slotted between the brutal Cobra and common GT, the newest Mustang was limited to a production run of 6500 for '03. A 4.6-liter V-8 provided 300 horses.

▶ A spring-mounted "shaker" hood scoop topped the Mustang Mach 1 V-8. Mach 1 prices started at $28,705.

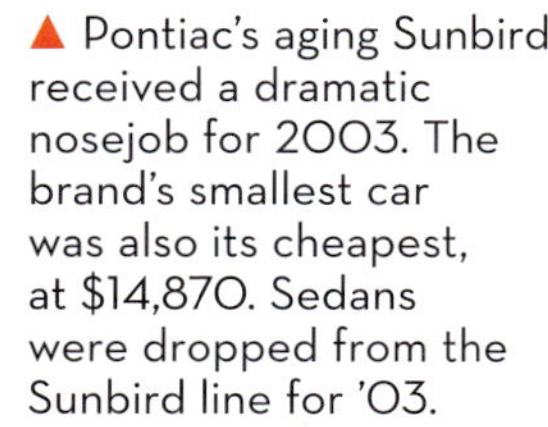

▲ Pontiac's aging Sunbird received a dramatic nosejob for 2003. The brand's smallest car was also its cheapest, at $14,870. Sedans were dropped from the Sunbird line for '03.

◄▼ Replacing the ancient S-10 line, Chevrolet's new Colorado small pickup was designed to be less truck-like and more commuter friendly. The top engine was a 220-horsepower inline five. Base price: $15,565.

► Chevy's Impala got a shot in the arm from the new line-topping SS model. Extroverted trim and an enhanced engine were part of the deal.

▼ Already popular with enthusiasts, Cadillac's CTS returned for 2004 with power borrowed from Chevy's Corvette. The CTS-V boasted a 400-horsepower 5.7-liter V-8, sportier suspension tuning, and unique trim all for the relatively low price of $49,995.

▼ Shaking off memories of Cadillac's ill-fated Allanté of the Eighties, GM's luxury division introduced the XLR roadster for 2004. Aimed squarely at the Mercedes-Benz SL convertible, XLR sported edgy styling and a folding steel top.

▲ It took 30 years, but Pontiac again struck on the magic combination of elements worthy of the GTO badge. Based on Holden of Australia's rear-drive Monaro coupe, the newest "Goat" boasted subtle styling and Corvette-sourced power. A six-speed manual transmission came standard.

2004

The Chevy Impala brought bold styling to sedans and their Colorado replaced the 5-10 line.

2005

Pontiac debuted the G6, a striking and versatile midsize sedan.

◀ ▼ The bow-tie brand's legendary sports car was redesigned for 2005. The new Corvette gained power, lost weight, and looked sleeker. The Corvette's 6.0-liter V-8 heart made 400 horsepower, and 400 pound-feet of torque. For the first time since 1963, the headlights were exposed.

▲ Supercar maker Saleen introduced the track-ready, street-legal S7 in 2000. For '05, new twin turbos increased horsepower to 750, and propelled the carbon-fiber beauty through the 0–60 mph sprint in a breathtaking 2.8 seconds. All the excitement of the S7's 7.0-liter V-8 could be yours for $555,000.

▲ Fleshing out the Mercury lineup for 2005 was Mariner, an up-content version of Ford's Escape compact SUV. A 3.0-liter V-6 was standard.

Without the division's trademark bodyside cladding, the Pontiac G6 was a clean break from the past. Replacing the ubiquitous Grand Am, G6 boasted an optional 3.9-liter V-6.

◀ Based on the same General Motors Theta architecture as Saturn's Vue, Chevrolet's new Equinox finally gave the brand a contemporary model for the entry-level SUV arena. A 3.4-liter V-6 was the only available engine.

▶ Chrysler's brash new 300 marked the return of the big American sedan. Base price: $23,595. The line-topping 300C carried a 5.7-liter Hemi V-8 and started at $32,370.

▶ Spicing up the already sexy Crossfire, Chrysler launched the potent SRT-6 edition for 2005. A supercharger upped the output of the standard 3.2-liter V-6 from 215 to 330 horsepower. Also new for 2005 was the Crossfire convertible, available in standard and SRT-6 trim. The aggressive rear spoiler and 15-spoke wheels shown here were part of the SRT-6 equipment list.

▲ A literal show car come to life, Solstice was Pontiac's answer to Mazda's evergreen Miata roadster. A 2.4-liter 170-horsepower "Ecotec" four was earmarked to provide motivation for the two-seater upon its debut in late 2005 as an '06 model.

▲ Saturn's Redlines were the top performers of their model lines. This 2005 Ion Redline boasted a supercharged engine, racy trim, and 17-inch wheels.

◀ Relay, Saturn's first minivan, was one of a quartet of new family haulers from General Motors. Sister ships Buick Terraza, Chevy Uplander, and Pontiac Montana SV6 all debuted for 2005.

◀ The low-slung and curvaceous Pontiac Solstice convertible whispered "sports car fun" to aficionados, but its coarse, 2.4-liter, 177-horse inline four couldn't deliver on the promise of Solstice's looks. Still, a $19,915 retail price for the base model was mightily appealing to many shoppers.

▲ Ford's aging Taurus was replaced by the crisply styled Fusion, a shot across the bows of segment leaders Accord and Camry. Fusion matched those rivals for interior room and road manners, but couldn't duplicate their overall refinement. The same plus and minus points characterized the similar Mercury Milan.

▲ Jeep based its new, 7-passenger Commander on the sportier Grand Cherokee. Commander's exterior lines were squared-up in the classic Jeep style, and the vehicle combined reasonable comfort and utility. Buyers with fat wallets and a love of option packages could drive off with a Commander costing $45,000.

◀ Impala was reskinned for 2006, and its cousin, the Monte Carlo (*left*) recieved fresh front sheet metal. Each was available in a high-performance SS model that included a 303-bhp 5.3-liter V-8. The Monte Carlo was discontinued after the 2007 model year.

2006

Dodge reintroduced the Charger. Technology became a major selling point.

◀ A venerated name from Dodge history was revived this season when the Charger bowed as a 4-door-sedan companion to the Magnum wagon. The two available V-6s were only adequate, but a pair of V-8s, particularly the 425-bhp, 6.1-liter mill, reminded drivers of past Charger glory. Retail price on the top SRT8 was $35,320.

2007

Ford introduced the Edge, a stylish crossover SUV with an emphasis on technology and comfort.

▲ Ford's Edge was a midsize sport-ute with a transversely mounted engine and available all-wheel drive. More than 130,000 were sold during calendar-year 2007, justifying Ford's commitment to the Edge's design and marketing.

▶ The decades-old association of Ford and Carroll Shelby was revived for '07, with the introduction of the Mustang Shelby GT500. The ponycar's top, normally aspirated V-8, at 4.6 liters, produced 319 horsepower; the 5.4-liter Shelby powerplant was supercharged, and unleashed 500 horses. A six-speed manual was mandatory.

▼ Fresh styling and more power marked GMC's Yukon line, including the luxury-class Denali (*shown*). Denali could accommodate up to eight passengers who rode in comfort, thanks to the standard Autoride suspension system. Other no-extra-cost goodies included OnStar, a power liftgate, and power-adjustable pedals.

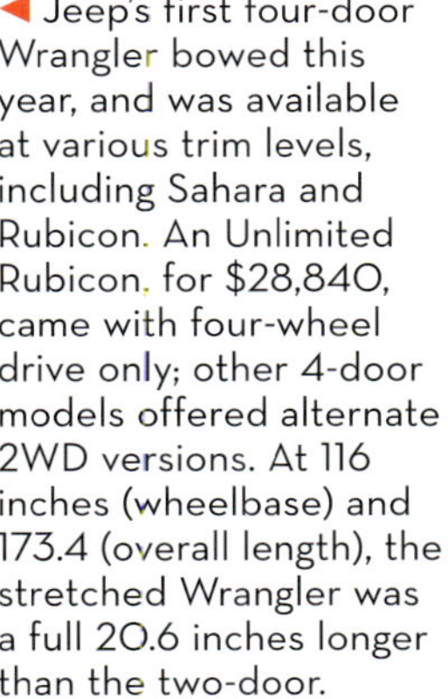

◀ Jeep's first four-door Wrangler bowed this year, and was available at various trim levels, including Sahara and Rubicon. An Unlimited Rubicon, for $28,840, came with four-wheel drive only; other 4-door models offered alternate 2WD versions. At 116 inches (wheelbase) and 173.4 (overall length), the stretched Wrangler was a full 20.6 inches longer than the two-door.

▶ Similar to the Pontiac Solstice, the Saturn Sky was a radical departure for a marque known mainly for pure and simple transportation. The top-level Red Line ran with a turbocharged, direct-injection 2.0-liter inline four rated at 260 horsepower. Thus equipped, acceleration was impressive; Saturn claimed 5.5 seconds for the 0–60 mph sprint.

◀ The composite body panels that had helped make Saturn unique were abandoned when the compact Vue SUV was redesigned. Based on GM's Europe-only Opel Antara, Vue had a well-finished interior and offered brisk acceleration with either of two available V-6s. An available gas/electric hybrid was naturally slower and could not run on electric power alone.

2008

The recession hit, hurting car sales. The auto industry faced a financial crisis.

◀ What Buick's midsize LaCrosse got for '08, the full-size Lucerne got, too: a go-gettem Super model. Lucerne's 4.6-liter V-8 was ordinarily rated at 275 bhp, but it produced 292 horses when upgraded for the Super. Neither flamboyant nor conservative, the Lucerne Super was a competitive addition to the big-car segment.

▶ GM's bowtie division went world-class that year with the smartly redesigned Malibu, the smaller of Chevy's midsize sedans (the other was the Impala). Crisp styling, fresh power, sensible interior layout, and a gas/electric Hybrid model made Malibu a car that could confidently take on Camry and Accord.

▼ The Roush Mustang was a track-ready, street legal aftermarket mod package to the Mustang GT. Upgrades to body, engine, and handling were so significant that Roush, rather than Ford, was the manufacturer of record. The GT's 300 horsepower was bumped to 430 on the Roush Stage 3, and to 435 on the 427R. Transmission choices were a 5-speed automatic or a 5-speed manual, with a short-throw shifter. Consumer Guide® testers characterized the 427R's acceleration as "brutally fast."

▼ At $109,000 to $128,500, the Tesla Roadster wasn't inexpensive—but then, how many purely electric cars could do the 0–60-mph dash in 3.7 seconds, or could be recharged overnight with a simple 120- or 240-volt plug-in? Tesla sales material promised a 236-mile range, and described one owner who managed 313 miles (driving pretty slowly) in Australia's Global Green Challenge.

▲ As Saturn approached the end of its life, it produced some of the best cars in its history. Astra, Saturn's replacement for the Ion as the marque's entry-level model, impressed observers for its value ($15,875 to start), fresh styling, and generally high level of materials and construction. The top-of-the-line XR could be had in 4- and 2-door body styles.

▼ The Dodge Caliber received a literal boost with the introduction of the sporty SRT4 turbo, priced to sell with a starting price of $22,435. That was a bargain, given that the blown 2.4-liter inline four was mated to a Getrag 6-speed manual transmission. Dodge claimed that the SRT4 did the 0–60 sprint in less than 6 seconds.

▼ The fabled Dodge Challenger returned from a four-decade hiatus as a 2008 model, with retro styling that captured the essence of the original. Top engine, a 425-horse 6.1-liter V-8, was reserved for the SRT8. In this guise, Challenger was a terror: brutally fast off the line and effortlessly quick on the highway. Buffs' only complaint was that no manual transmission was offered.

▲ Chrysler added a two-door convertible to the second-generation Sebring, the company's attractively priced midsize car. A soft top was standard, and a power-retractable hardtop was an available option. At $25,470 to start, the Sebring ragtop was a credible convertible choice, but lacked real refinement.

► The Avenger sat out the '07 model year, and was brought back by Dodge for 2008. As before, prices were appealing, starting at $18,590 for a stripped SE sedan. Avenger was likely to be more pleasing at higher trim levels, such as an AWD R/T sedan. But however you looked at it, the car had an unrefined drivetrain and a cheaply finished interior.

◄ Satisfactory levels of inventory, plus tweaks-in-progress, caused there to be no 2007 Dodge Viper—but when the car returned for 2008 it had an 8.4-liter V-10 that pushed out a scary 600 horsepower. (Previous hp was 510, from an 8.3-liter V-10.) As it had been from the beginning, Viper was essentially an engine with a seat: blisteringly fast (0–60 in less than 4 seconds), nervous in traffic, and noisy as all get-out. Viper fans swore by it.

▼ With the new GXP, Pontiac's sporty G8 added a highly capable performance sedan. A 6.2-liter V-8 cranked out 402 horsepower and 402 pound-feet of torque—potent enough to encourage Pontiac to claim a 0–60-mph time of 5.3 seconds. A GXP with an optional 6-speed manual suggests that the 5.3 figure was probably no pipe dream.

▲ Cadillac's most aggressive and unusual car, the low-slung, high-performance XLR entered its final season with freshened exterior styling. New 18-inch wheels adorned the Platinum model that replaced the previous base XLR. The top engine, a supercharged 4.4-liter V-8, carried on with 443 hp. XLR was based on the Corvette, and served its purpose by inviting new perceptions of the Cadillac brand.

Mix plentiful passenger and cargo room with an upright, retro-boxy body—sporting ribbed side doors and available contrasting color top, no less—and you had Flex, Ford's new entry in the midsize SUV segment. It was a head-turner that challenged the Dodge Journey, GMC Acadia, and Honda Pilot.

▼ As much a cultural statement as a hardworking truck, the hunky, redesigned Ram offered a composed, best-in-class ride and an increase in horsepower: now 390 (up from 345) with the top 5.7-liter Hemi V-8. Interior roominess and materials were first-rate, and cargo beds at a variety of lengths were available.

2009

GM and Chrysler received government bailouts. Hybrid and models gained popularity.

2010

The automotive industry saw a shift toward more fuel-efficient and environmentally friendly vehicles.

▼ The 2010 Mustang benefited from a modest restyle and improved cabin materials. GT's 4.6-liter V-8 was now rated at 315 horsepower.

▲ The $130K, all-electric 2010 Tesla Roadster improved on the '08 design with a more comfortable cockpit and better ergonomics, such as simple buttons (replacing a shifterlike stick) for park, reverse, neutral, and drive. Tesla claimed 236 miles on a single charge, which could be accomplished at a 220-volt outlet in as few as four hours. The roadster developed 288 horsepower from a 275-volt AC induction air-cooled electric motor. Base models ran 0–60 in 3.9 seconds; Sport iterations did it in 3.7—and in uncanny silence.

▲ Back in the 1970s, one of the signature colors of Dodge's Challenger was "Plum Crazy," which was resurrected for limited-edition versions of the 2010 Challenger R/T Classic (shown) and Challenger SRT8.

In addition to freshened styling and the new gas-electric hybrid, Fusion introduced a Sport model this year. It had a 3.5-liter V-6 that developed a robust 263 bhp.

▲ Midsize crossover practicality and luxury-style came via Lincoln's new MKT (base price range, $44,200 to $49,200), which was available in front-wheel or AWD iterations. Under the skin, MKT was based on the Ford Flex, and seated up to seven. At the high end, it could be had with a power-folding third-row seat and a refrigerated console box. Base engine was a 3.7-liter V-6 producing 270 bhp; the uplevel motor was a 3.5-liter EcoBoost V-6 producing 355 bhp.

◀ Ford's Taurus was redesigned for 2010. For the first time since 1999, a SHO performance variant was offered which used the new twin-turbocharged 3.5-liter V-6 EcoBoost engine rated at 365 horsepower. SHO also came standard with a 6-speed automatic transmission and all-wheel drive.

▶ Assemble Ford's SVT team. Take one Mustang GT fitted with a 5.4-liter V-8. Add supercharger and intercooler. Beef up the suspension, drop in a cool-air intake, and throw in an exclusive twin-disc clutch mated to a 6-speed manual. Install a modified front end designed to reduce drag, and an aluminum "power dome" hood. Mix all of this and you had the fastest Shelby GT500 yet, with 0–60 times in the 4-second range. The tweaked clutch smoothed takeoffs and shifts, making this Shelby reasonably tractable on the street. Top speed was electronically limited to 155 mph, but that wasn't likely to deter aftermarket tinkerers who wanted more. The car was available as a coupe and convertible, at prices that started at around $45,000.

▼ Corvette's Z51 option package went away this year and was replaced by the Grand Sport model, which slotted above the base 'Vette in a lineup that also included the faster Z06 and ZR1. Grand Sport had exclusive suspension tweaks, styling cues, and axle gearing. Standard GS engine was a 6.2-liter V-8 developing 430 horsepower and 424 pound-feet of torque.

◀ Camaro, one of the best-loved cars in Chevy history, returned with considerable fanfare for 2010. Retro-modern design captured the essence of the first-generation Camaro; likewise a trio of capable engines: a 3.6-liter V-6 rated at 304 hp (standard on Camaro LS and LT); a 6.2-liter V-8 with 405 hp (standard on SS with 6-speed automatic transmission); and a 426-horse version of the 6.2 (standard on SS with 6-speed manual).

2011

Car manufacturers focused on improving fuel efficiency and safety features, with an increase in hybrid and EV options.

▼ The world's first extended-range electric vehicle, the Chevy Volt went on sale in California and Michigan late in 2010, as a 2011 model. Additional markets were added for calendar-year '11. Volt was a four-passenger midsize 4-door hatchback with a unique feature: Unlike most gas-electric hybrids, the Volt's wheels were driven by electricity only. This was a plug-in car that could be charged overnight, and provided a 40-mile electric-only range. A 1.4-liter gas-fueled four generated electricity once the battery pack was depleted. Although clearly a specialty vehicle, Volt was critical to GM's attempts to recast itself as a world-class innovator.

◀ Dodge's lackluster midsize Avenger sedan received some welcome upgrades for 2011. Exterior styling was tweaked, and a redone interior offered improved materials. Engines were shared with Chrysler's 200. This year, available trim levels were base Express, mid-range Mainstreet, and top-line Lux.

▶ The midsize CTS was Cadillac's best-selling car, and for 2011 a racy 2-door coupe joined the 4-door sedan (*shown*) and station wagon versions. All three body styles were available as a high-performance CTS-V model which used Cadillac's supercharged 6.2-liter V-8 rated at 556 hp.

▲ Dodge also revamped the rear-drive Charger sedan for 2011. SE models used a 292-bhp 3.6-liter V-6, while the R/T (*shown*) had a 370-horsepower 5.7-liter Hemi V-8. All models used a 5-speed automatic, and R/Ts could be ordered with optional all-wheel drive.

◀ A convertible version of Chevy's new-for-2010 ponycar, the Camaro, arrived during the 2011 model year. The base 3.6-liter V-6 got a bump in horsepower, from 304 to 312. Other available engines—a 6.2-liter V-8 with 400 bhp and a 6.2 with 426 bhp—continued.

2012

The automotive market saw the rise of compact crossovers and small cars. Manufacturers continued to focus on eco-friendly technology.

► Ford brought back the legendary Boss 302 name for the 2012 Mustang. It was available in two versions, and the extra-limited Laguna Seca model (*shown*) was a dedicated track car that featured front brake cooling ducts and a not-quite-street-legal front splitter.

◄ Tesla added to its all-electric lineup with the 2012 Model S. It was a 4-door hatchback with seating for seven—five adults could sit in the first two rows of seats and two children rode in optional rear-facing jump seats located in the cargo area. The first production models were delivered at Tesla's factory in Fremont, California, in June 2012. All early cars were the Signature Performance version that listed for $105,400 before any available tax credits. The EPA estimated the Tesla's range at 265 miles.

▲ Chevrolet introduced the Sonic subcompact for 2012. It replaced the Aveo as Chevy's smallest car, but unlike that South Korean import, the Sonic was built in America. Four-door sedan and hatchback body styles were available.

► Chevy's Camaro added a new ZL1 model for 2012. It used a version of the Cadillac CTS-V's supercharged 6.2-liter V-8 rated at 580 horsepower. Other performance upgrades included 20-inch wheels, Brembo-brand brakes, Magnetic Ride Control suspension, and GM's driver-adjustable Performance Traction Management system. Unique exterior pieces included an aluminum hood with a vented carbon-fiber center section, and a front fascia with an integrated air splitter.

▼ Chevrolet's eight-passenger Traverse crossover received its first major updates for 2013. Exterior styling was revised, and the interior benefitted from upgraded materials. All models had a 3.6-liter V-6 engine mated to an automatic transmission. Prices started at $30,340.

▲ Ford introduced the compact C-MAX sport utility for 2013. Based on the Focus, the front-drive C-MAX was offered in hybrid and plug-in hybrid versions. The latter was called C-MAX Energi (*shown*), and Ford claimed it could go 620 miles on a single electric charge and a single tank of gas. In all-electric mode, it could travel up to 21 miles.

▲ In 2013, Chevrolet marked the Corvette's 60th anniversary along with the C6's final model year with the Corvette 427 Convertible Collector Edition. Basically, it was the first Z06 convertible and was only offered with the 505-horsepower 7.0-liter (427-cubic inch) LS7 engine and a 6-speed manual transmission. All 2013 'Vettes could be ordered with the 60th Anniversary Appearance Package that added Arctic White paint and Diamond Blue interior trim. Full-length Pearl Silver Blue racing stripes were available separately.

► The Chevy Spark minicar was new this year. Only offered as a 4-door hatchback, Spark had room for four passengers. Several bright colors including Salsa Red (*left*) and Jalapeno Green (*right*) helped grab attention on the road.

◄ Ford Fusion was also available in a gas-electric Hybrid model (*shown*), along with the Energi plug-in hybrid. Upgrades to the hybrid system included a new lithium-ion battery pack and a smaller 2.0-liter Atkinson-cycle four-cylinder engine.

2013

Ford and Chevrolet introduced redesigned models, edging technology and performance foward. Fuel efficiency grew across all categories.

The 2013 Dodge Dart was the first vehicle from Chrysler that was built on a chassis supplied by parent company Fiat. Based on the Alfa Romeo Giulietta, the front-wheel drive Dart was available with three different four-cylinder engines and came in five trim levels.

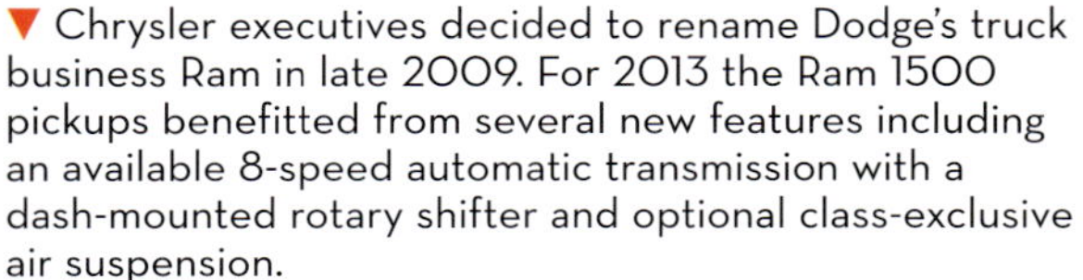

▼ Chrysler executives decided to rename Dodge's truck business Ram in late 2009. For 2013 the Ram 1500 pickups benefitted from several new features including an available 8-speed automatic transmission with a dash-mounted rotary shifter and optional class-exclusive air suspension.

▼ Although the ancient Crown Victoria platform went out of production in 2011, Ford didn't abandon the police-car market to Dodge's Charger and Chevy's Caprice. Instead, Ford offered the Taurus-based Police Interceptor, a partially purpose-built police cruiser available with a 3.5-liter 263-horsepower V-6 (in front-drive models) or a 3.5-liter EcoBoost twin turbo V-6 developing 365 horses that mated with AWD. Either engine was more powerful than the Crown Vic's V-8.

▲ Dodge Viper production had ended in July 2010, but the model returned as the SRT Viper for the 2013 model year. Available as a coupe in Viper and Viper GTS models, the new two-seater was powered by a 640-bhp 8.4-liter V-10 engine backed with a 6-speed manual gearbox. Top speed was a claimed 206 mph. Prices started at $97,395 for the base model and $120,395 for Viper GTS. After suffering from slow sales, the car was renamed Dodge Viper for 2015 and the base price was lowered to $84,995.

2014

The automotive industry embraced comprehensive technology with features like lane-keeping assist and adaptive cruise control.

▶ Cadillac introduced the ELR, an extended-range electric vehicle. In principle, ELR worked much like the Chevrolet Volt. Electric-only range was an estimated 37 miles, but once the battery was depleted the car's 1.4-liter four-cylinder engine generated electricity to power the car. Prices started at $75,995 before any available tax credits. Sales were slow.

▲ The 2014 Jeep Cherokee was based on the same Alfa Romeo-derived chassis as Dodge's Dart. Four-cylinder and V-6 engines were offered, and all used a new 9-speed automatic transmission. The Trailhawk (*shown*) was aimed at off roaders and included Jeep's Trail Rated branding.

▼ An all-new Corvette Stingray arrived for 2014. Chevy said it literally shared only a couple parts with the previous car. The new LT1 small-block V-8 was a 6.2-liter unit rated at 455 horsepower. With the optional Z51 Performance Pack, the Corvette could run 0–60 mph in 3.8 seconds.

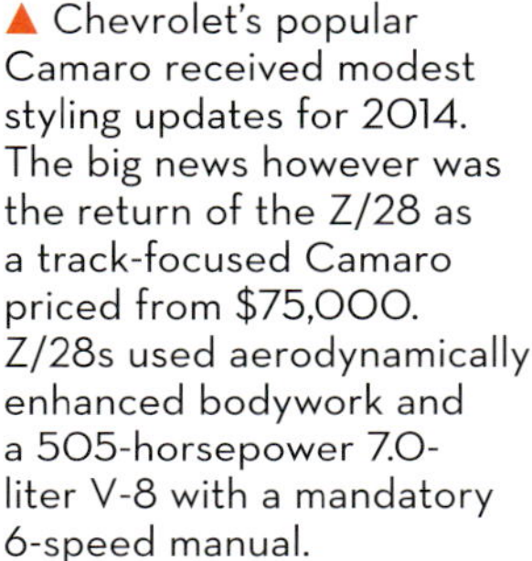

▲ Chevrolet's popular Camaro received modest styling updates for 2014. The big news however was the return of the Z/28 as a track-focused Camaro priced from $75,000. Z/28s used aerodynamically enhanced bodywork and a 505-horsepower 7.0-liter V-8 with a mandatory 6-speed manual.

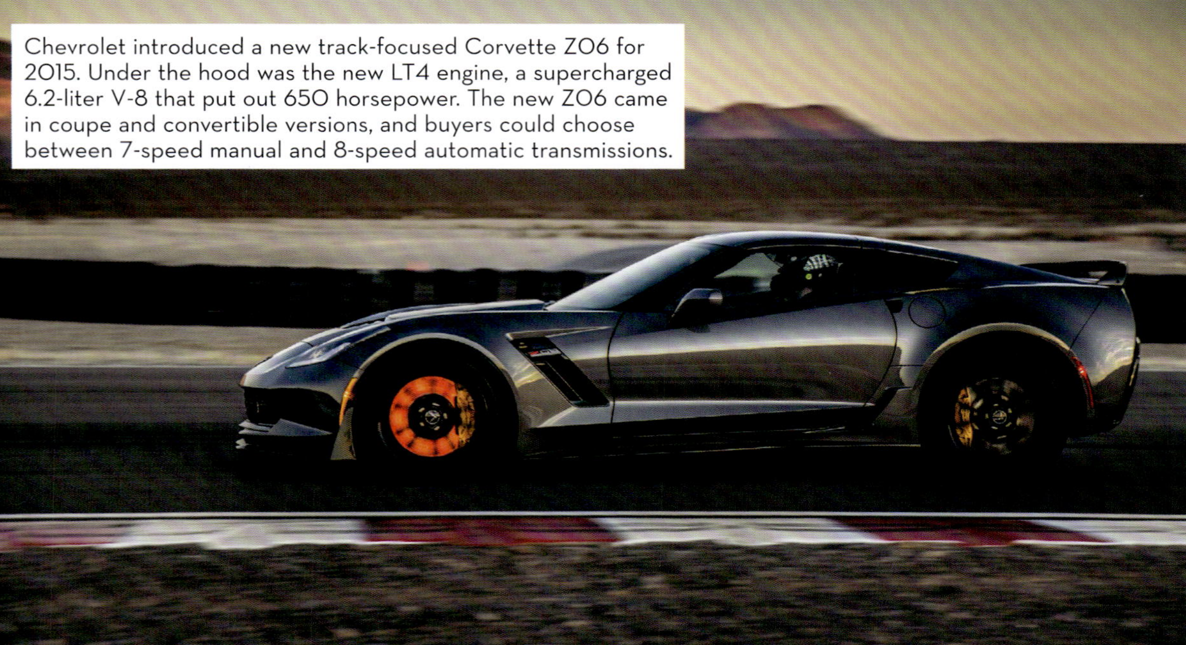

Chevrolet introduced a new track-focused Corvette Z06 for 2015. Under the hood was the new LT4 engine, a supercharged 6.2-liter V-8 that put out 650 horsepower. The new Z06 came in coupe and convertible versions, and buyers could choose between 7-speed manual and 8-speed automatic transmissions.

▲ Jeep entered the quickly growing small SUV segment with the 2015 Renegade. It was based on a Fiat-derived chassis and built in Italy. The off-road focused Trailhawk version (*shown*) carried Jeep's Trail Rated claim.

2015

The year saw the rise of EVs, with several models gaining popularity.

▲ Cadillac's Escalade was all-new for 2015. Standard (*shown*) and extended-wheelbase ESV variants of the body-on-frame SUV were offered. Prices started at $72,970.

◀ Like the short-lived Pontiac G8, the Chevrolet SS was an Americanized version of the Holden Commodore that GM built in Australia. Introduced as a 2014 model, the 2015 version added an optional 6-speed manual gearbox. The only engine was a 415-horsepower 6.2-liter V-8. With standard 6-speed automatic, Chevy claimed a 0–60 mph time of about 5 seconds.

◀ The 2015 Colorado was Chevrolet's new midsize truck. It came in base Work Truck (WT), LT, and off-road-inspired Z71 (*shown*) models. Extended cabs came with a six-foot-two-inch-long bed.

◀ Dodge Chargers wore freshened styling inside and out for 2015, but the big news was the SRT Hellcat. It was powered by a supercharged 6.2-liter Hemi V-8 rated at 707-horsepower mated to an 8-speed automatic. Almost unbelievably, the Charger could run the quarter mile in 11 seconds flat. Top speed was a claimed 204 mph. Charger SRT Hellcat priced from $63,995.

▲ Ford replaced the company's long-running E-Series vans with the new Transit. Two wheelbases, three body lengths, and three roof heights were available. In addition, customers could choose from cargo, passenger, and cutaway styles. Standard engine was a 3.7-liter V-6. Ford's popular 3.5-liter EcoBoost V-6 and a 3.2-liter 5-cylinder diesel engine were optional.

◀ Not wanting to miss the booming market for small SUVs, Chevy started importing the Trax in early 2015. A close cousin of Buick's popular Encore, the Trax ran a 1.4-liter turbocharged 4-cylinder engine rated at 138-horsepower.

▲ Dodge updated its Challenger coupes for 2015, but everything they did was completely upstaged by the SRT Hellcat. Once enthusiasts heard about its 707-horsepower supercharged Hemi, they had little interest in anything else. Unlike the automatic-only Charger version, Challenger Hellcats could also be ordered with a 6-speed manual transmission. Dodge claimed a stock Hellcat could run the quarter mile in 11.2 seconds. Base price was $59,995. Dodge literally could not make enough of them.

◀ Chevrolet debuted freshly designed versions of the Tahoe (*left*) and Suburban (*right*) full-size SUVs for 2015. These long-time favorites continued with body-on-frame construction. Each came in LS, LT, and top-line LTZ trim.

2016

Buick's 2016 Cascada marked the return of the convertible for the brand. With a smooth driving experience and high-tech features, it checked the boxes of many.

▲ Buick's first convertible in a quarter century was the 2016 Cascada. Based on GM's European-built Opel of the same name, the new open-air Buick had seating for four adults.

▲ The third-generation of the Cadillac CTS-V was introduced as a 2016 model. Announced only as a 4-door sedan, the new CTS-V boasted 640-horsepower from its supercharged 6.2-liter V-8. Other goodies included a carbon fiber hood and Brembo-brand brakes. Top speed was a claimed 200 mph.

Cadillac added a high-performance ATS-V to its lineup for 2016. Available in coupe (*shown*) and sedan body styles, the ATS-V had a 464-horsepower twin-turbocharged V-6 engine. Sedans priced from $61,460, while the coupe was $2200 more.

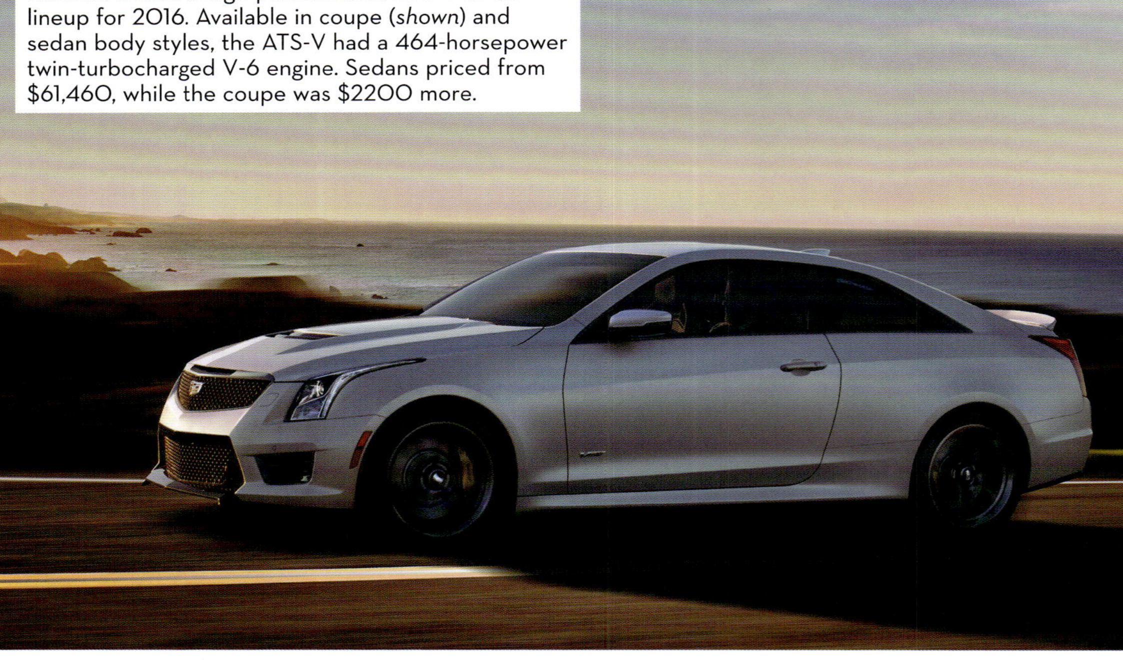

▼ An all-new Ford Focus RS was shown in Switzerland at the Geneva Auto Show in March 2015. Offering higher levels of performance than the Focus ST, the RS boasted a 2.3-liter EcoBoost four with at least 315-horsepower mated to a 6-speed manual gearbox.

▲Chevrolet's popular Equinox compact SUV was updated for 2016. Freshened exterior styling and a revised instrument panel were highlights.

► At the 2014 Los Angeles Auto Show, Ford rolled out a hotter version of the new Mustang wearing the legendary Shelby GT350 name. The street-legal GT350 was announced with a unique race-style 5.2-liter V-8 engine fitted with an exotic flat-plane crankshaft. Ford said the new engine would produce in excess of 500-horsepower. Other GT350 goodies included unique sheet metal forward of the windshield and cloth-covered Recaro bucket seats.

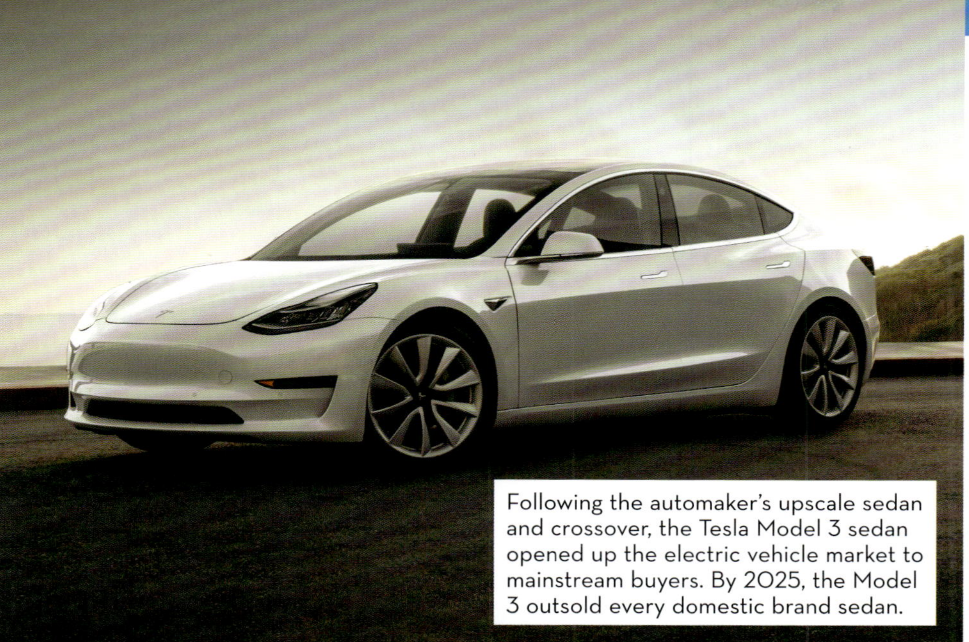

Following the automaker's upscale sedan and crossover, the Tesla Model 3 sedan opened up the electric vehicle market to mainstream buyers. By 2025, the Model 3 outsold every domestic brand sedan.

◀ Leading GM's charge into modern electrification, the Chevrolet Bolt EV carried the torch lit by the GM EV1 of the 1990s. With a starting price in the mid-$20,000 range, the Chevrolet Bolt became the first affordable domestic brand electric vehicle, and the best-selling EV in 2023 not called Tesla.

▲ Following the success of the 2004–2006 GT retro-themed sports car, Ford went back to the drawing board and created a ground-up homage to the 1960s Le Mans winner. In the modern Ford GT, a 647 hp turbocharged V-6 replaced the big V-8 found in the earlier editions as part of a limited production supercar with a claimed top speed of well over 200 mph.

◀ Karma Automotive was formed out of the bankruptcy of Fisker. The Karma Revero was formerly sold as the Fisker Karma and still featured Henrik Fisker's low, swoopy styling. An electric car by design, the Revero hid a four-cylinder gas engine to provide electricity to supplement the relatively small 21kW battery pack. Sales were slow.

▶ This stylish sedan attempted to revitalize Lincoln's passenger car lineup by invoking the classic nameplate. The tenth generation of the Continental was slightly shorter overall than the Lincoln MKS it replaced, but the clean modern design was all Lincoln.

2017

Tesla's Model 3 made electric cars more accessible with its affordable price and remarkable range.

▲ Ford's smallest crossover finally entered the U.S. market. Built in India, the subcompact EcoSport was offered with a 1.0L turbocharged three-cylinder or a 2.0L four with all-wheel drive optional. In the base trim level, the EcoSport was Ford's last model with a starting price under $20,000.

▲ Offered in two lengths, the full-sized, three-row Ford Expedition featured a surprisingly small—for such a big truck—3.5L turbo V-6 as its only engine choice but with 375 hp or 400 hp, depending on trim level. Off-road FX4 increased the SUV's capability and Pro Trailer Backup Assist improved towing.

▲ The Jeep Cherokee's controversial front and rear end designs disappeared for 2018 with a far more conventional look. Making the Cherokee blend in with the competition may not have been the best move, as sales fell quickly after the 2018 model's peak.

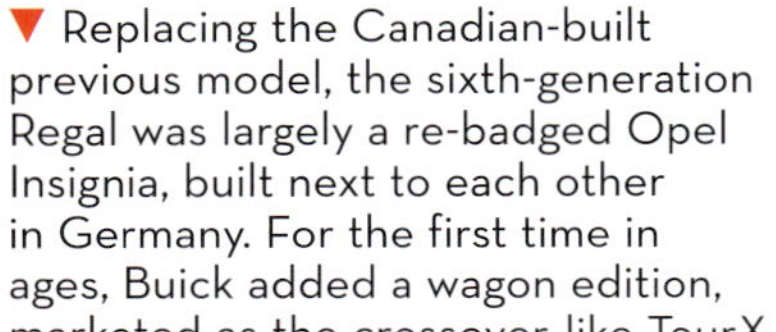

▼ Replacing the Canadian-built previous model, the sixth-generation Regal was largely a re-badged Opel Insignia, built next to each other in Germany. For the first time in ages, Buick added a wagon edition, marketed as the crossover-like TourX.

2018

Ford's EcoSport debuted in the U.S., introducing a high-quality SUV option.

Specially equipped for use on the drag strip, the Dodge Challenger SRT Demon featured a 6.2L version of the Hemi V-8 with a supercharger. The new package combined for 808 hp on pump gas and 840 hp on 100 octane fuel. Accelerating to 60 mph took only 2.3 seconds.

▼ The Jeep Wrangler was completely redesigned, not that one could easily tell. The previously flat grille bulged slightly for aerodynamic improvements and a new shoulder line was added to hide the thicker doors. While the V-6 remained, a new turbocharged four-cylinder joined the lineup which included a mild hybrid system called eTorque.

▲ Updated styling with revised front and rear lighting went with the full-sized sedan's comfortable ride. Powertrain options on the Cadillac XTS ranged from a 304 hp front-wheel drive model to the V-Sport edition with 410 hp and all-wheel drive.

▼ All new styling brought about a more upscale look to the Navigator for 2018. Clean lines, big wheels, and Lincoln's new mesh grille combined to make the premium SUV fit in with the global competition. Standard power topped 450 hp from its relatively small V-6.

▲ Cadillac's flagship sedan carried over largely unchanged with one important exception. The CT6 introduced the $5,000 SuperCruise option that provided semi-autonomous driving across 130,000 miles of mapped highways. Quarterly updates improved the system's range to provide hands-free driving.

2019

Automakers continued to create more hybrids and electric models. SUVs and crossovers remained dominant.

◀ Positioned as the entry-level Cadillac crossover, the four-cylinder five-seater XT4 targeted small BMW, Audi, and Mercedes-Benz models but without the successful execution of their German counterparts. Sales, however, easily topped the European competitors.

▲ Production of the Cadillac CT6-V Blackwing started and stopped very quickly with only about 1,400 units built. Under the hood was an all-new 4.2L DOHC twin-turbo V-8 with up to 550 hp. To make the big sedan more athletic, engineers kept the weight down, allowing it to shoot to 60 mph in just over four seconds.

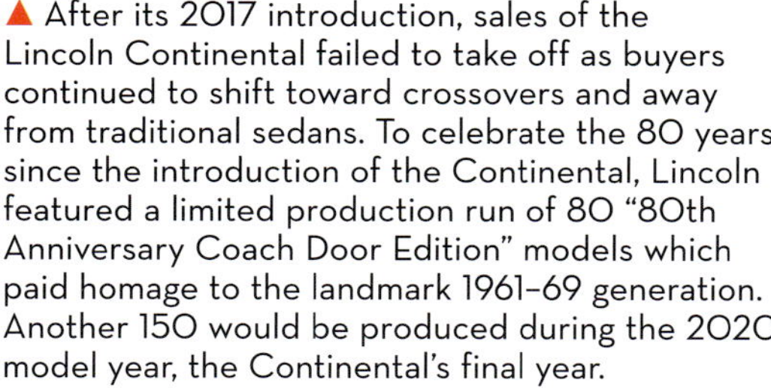

▲ After its 2017 introduction, sales of the Lincoln Continental failed to take off as buyers continued to shift toward crossovers and away from traditional sedans. To celebrate the 80 years since the introduction of the Continental, Lincoln featured a limited production run of 80 "80th Anniversary Coach Door Edition" models which paid homage to the landmark 1961–69 generation. Another 150 would be produced during the 2020 model year, the Continental's final year.

◀ With the popularity of the Wrangler, adding a pickup seemed like a great extension to the Jeep lineup. Reviving the Gladiator name, the new pickup appealed to buyers not looking for a full-sized truck but needing something more utilitarian than a four-door SUV. The rugged Gladiator ticked all those boxes.

▶ Replacing the ATS, the Cadillac CT4 took over as the entry-level model in the lineup. Powered by a four-cylinder or V-6 engine, the CT4 had optional all-wheel drive and a top-of-the-line 325 hp CT4-V trim level. Pricing started at just under $34,000.

▲ The larger sibling to the CT4, the CT5 replaced the long-running CTS sedan. Priced nearly $4,000 more than the smaller model, the CT5 became the most popular Cadillac passenger car but continued to sell well behind the brand's SUVs and crossovers as buyers continued to shift away from sedans.

◀ Settling in above the two-row XT5, Cadillac's full-sized XT6 offered a third row and seating for up to seven. Boxier in design than the smaller crossovers, the XT6 was more useful with a larger cargo area when the third row was dropped. A good seller in the U.S., the XT6 was even more popular in China.

▲ Styled distinctively different than the light-duty version, the Chevrolet Silverado HD featured a bold front end with large CHEVROLET letters embossed across the nose. Plenty of cameras throughout helped with trailer towing and parking. A choice of gas or diesel engines tailored the truck for any purpose.

▲ After a brief U.S. run following the demise of Plymouth two decades earlier, the Chrysler Voyager minivan returned as the entry-level variant of the Pacifica. Replacing the former L and LX trim levels of the Pacifica, the Voyager was almost imperceptibly different than its more expensive variant. The Voyager name would be dropped from consumer versions after the 2021 model and offered only to fleets.

▼ With almost all of the cars out of the Ford lineup, a softer, more rounded Ford Escape appealed to buyers who once bought a Focus or Fusion. The $26,130 base model started with a turbo three-cylinder, front-wheel drive, and a fully digital instrument panel but offered options including all-wheel drive and a 250 hp four.

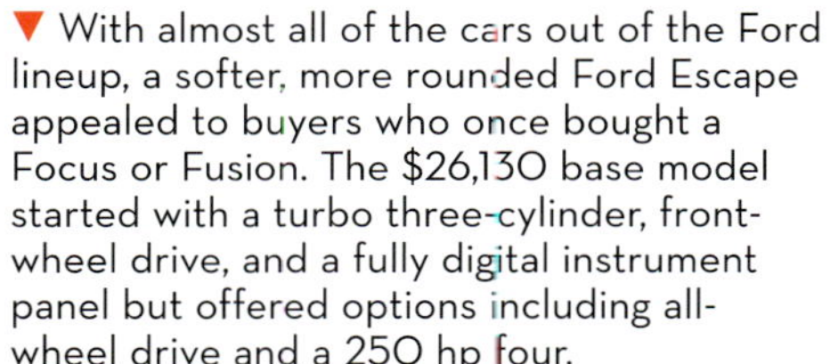

2020

Production slowed as the pandemic disrupted the industry. Demand for trucks and SUVs remained high.

◀ Replacing the compact MKC, Lincoln's all-new Corsair focused on the brand's "quiet luxury" theme with its smooth exterior lines and improved driver experience. "Symphonic chimes" replaced the traditional alert sounds, the new interior was designed for "visual calmness," and the Revel sound system spread 14 speakers around the interior.

▲ A mild exterior refresh of the Ford Transit accompanied a new interior and upgraded drivetrains. High on the dash was a useful 4-inch or optional 8-inch infotainment screen. A 275 hp V-6 became standard with a twin-turbo V-6 and 10-speed automatic with all-wheel drive optional.

▶ Styled differently than the light-duty version, the GMC Sierra HD sported a big grille across a modern and attractive front-end. Even in the top Denali trim, the all-new model was not quite as luxurious as the similarly trimmed Ram offering, an error which would be corrected on future models.

▲ Taking the lead from the Model 3, the Tesla Model Y pierced the crossover market with its electric silence and a starting price of $51,190. Buyers snapped up the tall five-passenger utility. Subsequent price reductions and additional assembly plants would make the Model Y the most popular crossover in the U.S by 2022 and the most popular vehicle in the world by 2023.

2021

The Ford Bronco officially returned, challenging Jeep's Wrangler. Chevrolet finally started building mid-engined Corvettes.

After decades of hints, the mid-engined Corvette finally entered production in early 2020. Keeping only the pushrod V-8 and general design theme, the "eighth generation" Corvette aimed directly at the Italian exotics. A DOHC 5.5L engine powered the Z06 edition starting in 2023 with the hybridized and all-wheel drive E-Ray joining the lineup for 2024.

▲ Reviving the long-running model name after being dormant for a quarter century, the Ford Bronco focused on the market long dominated by the Jeep Wrangler. Offered in two-door or four-door body styles, hardtop and soft-top editions were available and a plethora of accessories allowed owners to personalize each truck. Strong name recognition encouraged Ford to introduce a Bronco Sport crossover for more mainstream drivers.

▲ As part of the Bronco lineup, the compact Bronco Sport offered the off-road image and a degree of its capability to a wider market. With its lighter-duty suspension, the Bronco Sport targeted suburban use rather than hardcore trailblazing.

▼ Upping the ante once again, the Dodge Charger received the SRT Hellcat Redeye trim level, which included the Hellcat's widebody and increased the output of the supercharged 6.2L Hemi V-8 to an amazing 797 hp. It was a relative bargain with a starting price of $75,820.

◀ Filling the gap left by the lack of a Shelby edition, the Ford Mustang Mach 1 was powered by a 480 hp version of the 5.0L Coyote V-8. Some Shelby's suspension parts made the transition and buyers had the choice of 6-speed Tremec manual or 10-speed automatic transmissions.

▲ At the top of the Silverado line, the new ZR2 trim level was added. Taking cues from the Colorado ZR2, the Silverado got electronic-locking differentials and Multimatic-supplied DSSV dampers for improved off-road capability. A larger 13.4-inch touchscreen and SuperCruise were newly available on various Silverado trims.

▶ The Buick Enclave's updated exterior featured new LED headlights and taillights. Inside, the three-row crossover received a new center console with transmission selector buttons instead of a shift lever. Other improvements included a new steering wheel and wireless Apple CarPlay and Android Auto.

▼ With the performance-oriented CT4-V already on the road, Cadillac upped the ante with its Blackwing edition. Output of the 3.6L twin-turbo V-6 increased to 472 hp, the improved suspension helped keep the power on the road, and Brembo brakes brought it back down from speed. Starting price was $59,990.

◀ The big brother to the CT4-V Blackwing, the CT5-V Blackwing harnessed the supercharged 6.2L V-8 from the Corvette. Mated to 6-speed manual or 10-speed automatic, the big 668 hp engine could move the sedan to sixty in as little as 3.4 seconds with a claimed top speed of over 200 mph.

2022

EVs gained momentum as new models hit the market. Rivian expanded production of its all-electric trucks and SUVs.

▶ Hitting the streets after the pickup, the Rivian R1S SUV, with its clean lines and room for up to seven passengers, opened new markets for the startup automaker. The fully electric R1S provides up to 835 hp with the available quad-motor edition.

2023

EV-dominance continued to surge. Manufacturers worked to refine their offerings to compete in a dynamic market.

▼ Reengineered, the Chevy Colorado received all new styling. Instead of the previous range of engines, the new model was exclusively powered by GM's turbo 2.7L four with up to 310 hp. A new interior featured an 8-inch instrument cluster and 11.3-inch infotainment display. Five trim levels included the off-road ZR2.

▲ In addition to the 70th Anniversary Special Edition, the Corvette regained the Z06 trim level. Behind the seats sat an all-new DOHC 5.5L V-8 engine. With its flat-plane crankshaft, the new engine developed 670 hp without the help of turbos or a supercharger.

▼ Acquired by GM, Cruise developed autonomous driving technologies. Their first dedicated model was the Cruise Origin, a box-shaped people carrier that required no driver. While a handful were produced, full production was indefinitely postponed.

With the industry moving toward full electrification, Cadillac couldn't be left behind. Cadillac's first electric model was the Lyriq crossover. All-new, the Lyriq was the first vehicle built on GM's "Ultium" electric platform and offered up to 500 hp.

▼ Taking its place at the top of the lineup, the $149,990 Cadillac Escalade-V got all of the bells and whistles. Instead of the truck-based engines, the Escalade-V borrowed its supercharged 682 hp 6.2L V-8 from the Corvette and added Brembo brakes and its own tuned suspension to create the ultimate SUV. For those looking for more room, the long-wheelbase Escalade-V ESV was also available.

▲ Pushing its coupe to the limit, Dodge Challenger SRT Demon 170 enhanced the supercharged Hemi V-8 to get 1025 hp out of it. Pricing it at $96,666 made it seem affordable; however, only 3000 would be available to U.S. buyers. It was also the final Challenger built in this generation.

▲ Ohio-based electric truck startup Lordstown Motors started production of its Endurance pickup at a former GM plant. Featuring four hub-mounted motors, the Lordstown Endurance claimed 600 hp and a range of up to 250 miles on a charge. After production of just 450 units, the company filed for bankruptcy in 2023.

▼ Updates to the Ford Escape included new headlights and grille on the outside. A new digital instrument cluster and an optional 12.3-inch screen provided access to many infotainment controls. Hybrid and plug-in hybrid models were reengineered for better fuel economy.

◀ Henrik Fisker launched another company to market electric vehicles, this time starting with a crossover, the Ocean. The stylish utility vehicle rolled off assembly lines in Austria and made their way to the U.S. just in time for the company to go bankrupt. About half of the total production of 10,142 were sold in the States.

◀ Reviving the old Hudson and AMC nameplate, the Dodge Hornet moved the brand into the compact crossover market. Similar to the Alfa Romeo Tonale, the Italian-built Hornet offered Dodge's sporty trim and the brand's first plug-in hybrid drivetrain. With a starting price of over $30,000, sales were slow.

▶ The first hybrid Corvette, the E-Ray added an electric motor to the front axle, making it also the first production Corvette with all-wheel drive. Capable of driving in fully-electric mode for up to 45 miles, when all propulsion systems were engaged, including the 6.2L V-8, 655 hp got the coupe or convertible to 60 mph in 2.5 seconds.

▼ With its polarizing design, the Tesla Cybertruck quickly became the best-selling electric pickup, passing the Ford F-150 Lightning and Chevrolet Silverado EV. Its slab-sided stainless-steel body and integrated bed gave it a look that cannot be confused with any other vehicle on the road anywhere on the planet.

▼ All-new and distinct from the gas-powered model with the same name, the Chevrolet Blazer EV was offered in rear-wheel drive or allwheel drive variants. Up to 288 hp was provided with a range of up to 279 miles on a single charge, positioning the Blazer EV in the middle of the crossover market.

▲ Introduced for the 2024 model year, the Dodge Charger broke from its previous generation by not including the Hemi V-8 engine. Replacing the former Challenger, the Charger two-door was the first modern electric model offered by Dodge with three motors powering all four wheels. For buyers not ready for an electric muscle car, the Charger also had a turbocharged six-cylinder with no less than 420 hp on tap. Among the highlights were its "Fratzonic Chambered Exhaust" helping bridge the gap from the Hemi's thunderous roar to the near silence of electric motors.

2024

Tesla's Cybertruck hit the streets after much anticipation. From end to end, it challenged the traditional conventions of trucks.

2025

American cars continued evolving with electric, hybrid, and performance models coexisting. Automakers focused on balancing tradition with future innovation.

▶ To complement the gas-powered models in the lineup, the Cadillac IQ featured a 200kWh battery pack to energize motors front and rear. Cadillac promised up to 460 miles on a single charge and filled the SUV with a 55-inch curved digital display and all the technology offered in other Escalade models.

▶ Inspired by the Jeep Wrangler, the Jeep Recon rode on a new platform designed to be electric. With its removable doors, the new EV planned to do what its big brother could but without a drop of gas.

▲ The ultimate Mustang took what Ford learned on the track and funneled it into one, low-production $300,000+ coupe. Upfront sat a supercharged 5.2L DOHC V-8 producing more than 800 hp. That power was pushed to the 8-speed dual clutch transaxle mounted at the rear to help balance the car for road racing.

While the Lyriq crossover became Cadillac's first electric model, the Celestiq sought to revive the classic era of the brand. This highly exclusive and fully electric model allows owners to add their specific touches and, with its price in excess of $300,000, chances are unlikely that any two will be identical.

▲ Starting with the Z06's DOHC V-8, the Chevrolet Corvette ZR1 added two turbochargers to increase the engine's output to an astounding 1064 hp. As the most powerful production Corvette ever, performance was promised to include a top speed in excess of 215 mph. New styling touches included the split rear window reminiscent of the famed 1963 model.